F·A·S·H·I·O·N

extras

Marshall Cavendish

Editor: Diana Mansour
Designer: Caroline Dewing

Published by
Marshall Cavendish Books Limited
58 Old Compton Street
London W1V 5PA

© Marshall Cavendish Limited 1986

ISBN 0 86307 445 6

Typeset by Bookworm Typesetting, Manchester
Printed and bound in Italy by L.E.G.O. Spa, Vicenza

C·O·N·T·E·N·T·S

I·N·T·R·O·D·U·C·T·I·O·N

Whether you enjoy knitting, dressmaking or embroidery, or would like to experiment with one of the slightly more unusual crafts such as fabric painting or leatherwork, there is something here for you. While some projects, such as the Fair Isle scarf (p71) or the cutwork leather belt (p46), require a certain degree of skill, many are very easy to make and rely for their effect on a firm, elegant design and a flair for colour.

The book is divided into six chapters: bags; belts and braces; collars, ties and scarves; headgear; footwear, and jewellery, and each one is filled with ideas. Some of them, such as twisted braid belts, frivolous bow ties or glitter on shoes, can be run up or painted on in a matter of minutes, adding an extra touch of fun or glamour – or both – to party clothes. Other projects such as the elegant suede clutch bag (p12) or the ritzy little cocktail hats (pp82-7) will take somewhat longer to make but are well worth the effort.

If you have no clear idea of what you want to make, one of the best ways to use this book is to glance through it and then take a good long look through your wardrobe. The chances are that it will contain quite a few clothes that you constantly reject as too dull or lacking a certain something, or because they have an unfashionable trim or you don't have the right belt or bag.

Take these out, decide what is needed to bring them back into fashion, and then the fun can start. It may well be that you will want to alter the colourway of a bag, belt or scarf to match a particular outfit, or change a motif to echo a patterned fabric, but you will certainly find plenty of ways to revitalize old clothes or add chic finishing touches to new ones.

Chapter 1

B·A·G·S

Bags are expensive, and if you want to have one for every occasion and each outfit and still have money left to put in your purse, the answer is to make your own. A smart pig-suede clutch bag, an embroidered bag for a summer's day, Victorian beaded purses, a host of pretty evening bags, as well as everyday bags to brighten up your shopping – there is plenty here for even the most demanding taste, plus a couple specially for children. So forget about safe, dull colours and transform your wardrobe by making a complete range of daytime and evening bags.

Suede bag

This smart suede clutch bag is made from one skin and finished with a zip opening on the inside and a purchased kilt buckle.

You will need: 9ft of pig suede, 40cm x 40cm lining, a 23cm zip, a kilt buckle, matching thread, fabric adhesive, a ballpoint machine needle, dressmaker's weights and carbon paper, and a small hammer covered with suede at the head.

Scale up main pattern from the grid. Trace off front flap section and outlines for lining to make separate patterns. Trace shapes for contrasting strips A and B and add 1.5cm seam allowances on each long edge.

Mark the outlines of the main pattern piece and flap pattern piece on the suede side of the skin, using dressmaker's carbon paper and holding it in place with weights. Cut out. Cut out contrasting strips A and B from the smooth side of the skin.

Mark a line 23cm long at centre of width, 4cm in from lower edge of bag

for zip opening. Cut along line to within 5mm of each end, then cut diagonally to corners. Glue edges of opening and fold 5mm to wrong side on each edge and triangles to wrong side at each end. Stick.

Glue right side of zip tape and place face down on wrong side of opening. Allow to dry, then stitch around edge of opening from right side.

Turn seam allowances to wrong side on top and bottom edges of contrasting strips A and B and stick. Glue again, position on right side of bag and make two rows of stitching 5mm apart along top and bottom edges.

Place buckle section of kilt buckle at centre of strip B with bottom of strap to middle of strip and buckle towards lower edge. Stitch.

Cut out lining, cut zip opening as before and press edges to wrong side.

Place on bag at position indicated with wrong sides together. Slipstitch lining to zip tape around zip opening.

Glue outer edges of bag and turn 1.5cm seam allowance to wrong side, over raw edges of lining. Gently hammer edge to flatten.

Glue side and front edges of separate front flap section, leaving long straight edge free. Turn 1.5cm to wrong side and hammer flat. Allow to dry. Glue all edges and stick to wrong side of main piece, overlapping raw edge of lining.

Glue seam allowances at side and lower edges of lining and fold the lower section to the centre along the fold line. Stick. Allow it to dry and stitch the layers together along top straight edge of pouch. Make two rows of topstitching 5mm apart around outer edges of bag. Stitch the top section of the kilt buckle to the point of the flap to fasten.

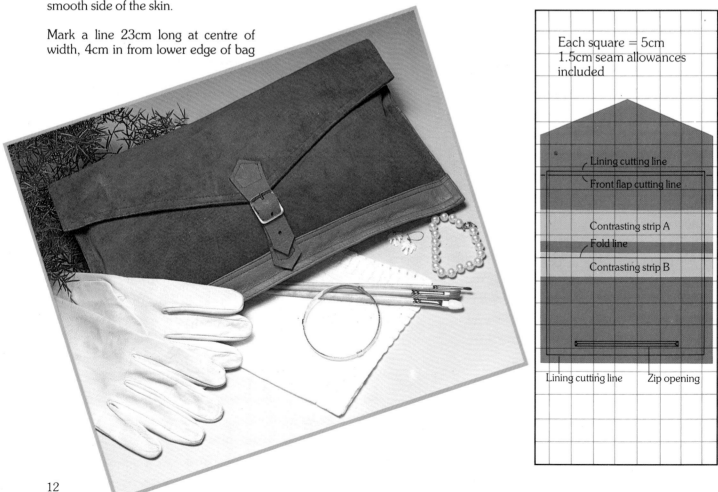

Each square = 5cm
1.5cm seam allowances included

Lining cutting line
Front flap cutting line
Contrasting strip A
Fold line
Contrasting strip B
Lining cutting line   Zip opening

Embroidered bag & belt

A summer garden party or an informal lunch would be perfect occasions for pretty accessories like these.

For the bag you will need: 1.5m of 7cm-wide woven carpet tape, 25cm x 50cm each of lining fabric and non-woven interfacing, and a selection of wools, cottons and embroidery silks.

Cut three 47cm strips of carpet tape and join them along the long edges. Cut out a piece of interfacing the same size as the bag fabric. Cut out a similar piece of lining the same size as the bag fabric plus 1cm all round for seams. Turn under and press the seam allowance of the lining fabric.

Working on the right side of the bag fabric, and using the photograph as a guide, embroider flowers and leaves along the joins and across one short edge of the fabric using toning and mixed coloured threads.

Turn under and press 1cm across the two short edges of the bag fabric. Tack and stitch the interfacing and the lining to the wrong side of the bag fabric. Turn up 16cm of the bag fabric and slipstitch the sides neatly. Fold over the top flap of the bag and press under a damp cloth.

For the belt you will need: a length of 7cm-wide woven carpet tape, the same length of lining and non-woven interfacing, a buckle, and the same selection of threads as for the bag.

Cut the tape to fit your waist plus an allowance for fitting the buckle.

Embroider leaves and flowers to match those on the bag.

Cut a piece of lining the same size as the belt plus 1cm all round. Turn under and press the seam allowances. Cut a piece of interfacing the same size as the belt and slip under the turnings of the lining fabric. Tack and slipstitch the lining to the belt.

Press well, gather the ends of the belt, if required, and fit the buckle.

Raffia shoulder bag

Overlap two triangles of woven raffia to make a comfortable shoulder bag finished with contrast binding and a toggle closure.

You will need: 80cm of 90cm-wide fine woven raffia, 80cm of 90cm-wide, off-white cotton fabric for lining, 3.50m of 25mm-wide green bias binding, 1.50m of 8mm-diameter filler cord for strap, four extra large metal eyelets, one wooden toggle, green stranded embroidery cotton and sewing thread.

Enlarge the pattern piece to scale, using dressmaker's graph paper. Cut out two pieces in raffia and two in lining fabric.

Tack lining to raffia, aligning raw edges and sewing close to the edge. Tack and machine stitch binding over raw edges of the two sides of each triangle, easing binding round curve at apex. Leave the base of each piece unbound.

Insert the eyelets at the positions indicated, following the manufacturer's instructions.

Fold each triangle in half along fold line. Overlap the sides of one triangle over the other, aligning edges at base. Tack base through all thicknesses. Slipstitch binding to raffia along overlapping edges on both the outer and inner surfaces.

Cut two 40cm lengths of bias binding and join along lengthwise folds to make a double width binding for the bottom edge of the bag. Stitch over raw edges, tucking in the ends and slipstitching the binding together at the sides of the bag.

For the strap, encase filler cord in bias binding, using a zipper foot to stitch close to cord. Cut cord slightly shorter than binding at each end, tuck in ends and slipstitch together. Thread each end through top then bottom eyelet and finish with a Chinese ball button (see page 29).

Sew the wooden toggle to the base of the V at the centre front of the bag, with stranded cotton. Cut a 15cm length of binding and fold it in half and in half again to make a narrow strip. Stitch along each edge and sew it to the inside of the back of the bag at the base of V to make a loop. Slip over toggle to close.

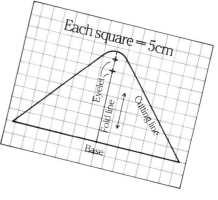

Each square = 5cm

Eyelet · Fold line · Cutting line · Base

Shopping bag

This shopping bag is made from PVC-coated fabric, so it is water-resistant as well as pretty. A firm cardboard base gives it added strength.

You will need: 70cm of 120cm-wide PVC-coated fabric (allow extra for matching pattern if required), matching polyester thread, 27cm x 15cm of stiff cardboard, PVC adhesive, No.14/90 sewing machine needle and some paper clips.

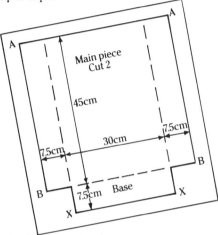

Following the diagram draw out paper pattern for main piece. On the wrong side of PVC arrange position of two main pieces side by side. Mark out two handles 11cm x 36cm below main pieces, and one base cover 33cm x 21cm beside main pieces. Cut out all pieces (1.5cm seam allowances are included).

Adjust machine to a long stitch. If, when stitching the right side of the PVC it tends to stick, sprinkle the surface lightly with talcum powder to help it to pass smoothly through the sewing machine.

With right sides facing, stitch main pieces together across base, X to X. Open seam and glue turnings down flat. In the same way, stitch side seams, A to B.

With right sides facing, arrange corners of base so seams at point B and X match and raw edges are level. Stitch across corners of base.

Around top edge fold 1cm, then a 4cm hem, over to the wrong side and hold

in place with paper clips. Stitch hem in place, removing paper clips as you go. Turn bag right side out.

With wrong sides together, fold main pieces along edges of side panels indicated by dashed lines. Topstitch along fold from hem to base to hold fold in place.

Fold seam allowances to wrong side along long edges of handles. With wrong sides facing, fold handles in half lengthwise, holding in place with paper clips. Topstitch along both long edges.

Underlap ends of handles to inside of top hem with inner edges of handles 8cm apart. Machine or backstitch ends of handles in place with a square of stitching.

Place cardboard centrally to wrong side of base cover. Fold edges of PVC over to other side of card and trim the corners to mitres. Glue them in place. Insert card, PVC side up, into the base of the bag.

Duffle bag

Youngsters will love this brightly coloured PVC duffle bag with attached miniature duffle purse. It's practical and fun.

You will need: 50cm of 110cm-wide green PVC-coated fabric, 30cm of 90cm-wide yellow PVC-coated fabric, 1m of thick white cord, 50cm of thin white cord, two D-rings, two dog-lead clips, green and yellow thread, bodkin and pinking shears.

Cut out one of each piece, pinking edges with shears. Cut two of E. With right side uppermost and lower edges level, topstitch A to B, using yellow thread. With right sides facing, stitch sides of A and B together, taking 1.5cm seam and leaving 2.5cm gap 11.5cm from top for cord.

Turn top of bag to wrong side along fold line. Make a channel for the cord by stitching two layers together with double rows of topstitching 4cm and 6.5cm from fold line.

With right sides facing, stitch ends of strip C together and then stitch to base D, taking 1.5cm seams.

Place pinked edge of C over lower edge of A and B, with side seams matching. With wrong side uppermost, insert base of tag E between the two sections at the side seam. Topstitch with yellow thread.

Thread tag through D-ring, fold down and topstitch free end to bag with a triangle of stitching.

Thread thick cord through channel using bodkin and then take through dog-lead clip. Knot ends together. Clip on to D-ring.

Thread second tag through D-ring and topstitch in place at top of one of the yellow triangles at side of bag, just below channel.

Make the duffle purse in the same way, omitting the tags and taking 1cm seams. Thread the thinner cord through the channel and second dog-lead clip. Attach it to the tag at the side of the main bag.

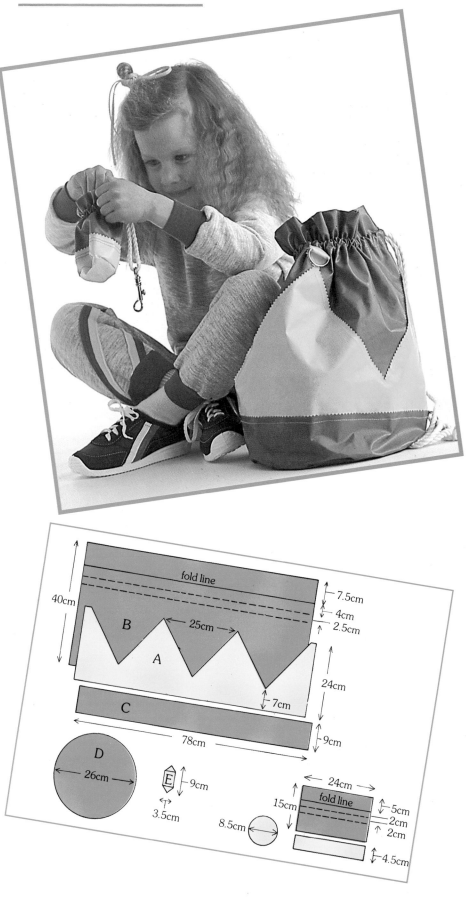

Child's shoulder bag

Make this cheerful bag for a child and you should end up with two smiling faces!

You will need: 50cm of 90cm-wide pink cotton fabric, scraps of blue and white cotton fabrics, 15cm and 20cm pink zips, brown and pink sewing thread, and two D-rings.

Cut three 22cm-diameter circles from pink fabric, two 4cm-circles from white and two 1.5cm-circles from blue. Use the white and blue circles for eyes and appliqué them to one pink circle. Draw in eyelashes and the nose and machine zigzag stitch along the lines.

Draw a 16cm mouth and cut it open. Snip into the corners, turn under and press 2mm at sides of the mouth. Tack a 15cm red zip behind the mouth and stitch in place. Press well and stitch the face to the second pink fabric circle.

Cut a 42cm x 6cm strip for the gusset, a 90cm x 8cm strip for the strap and two 25cm x 4cm strips for the top zipped sections of the gusset.

Fold the strap in half, stitch along the length, turn, press and topstitch close to the edge. Cut two 10cm lengths from the strap, thread each with a D-ring, and stitch the ends together.

Turn under and press 1cm along one long edge of each zip gusset piece, stitch to zip. Stitch the ends of the zip gusset to the 42cm gusset strip and sandwich the D-ring tabs in seams. Match the centre of the top zipped gusset to the top of the appliquéd side of the bag and stitch in place. Stitch the second side of the bag to gusset.

Thread the ends of the strap though D-rings and stitch in place.

Beach bag

Make a smart bag to hold your swimwear and sunbathing equipment, and co-ordinate it with your beachwear.

You will need: 60cm of 122cm-wide fabric (if it has a motif, make sure it falls in the centre or slightly below), 80cm of 90cm-wide white lining fabric, 20cm of 90cm-wide red cotton fabric, 90cm of piping cord No.3, 2m of piping cord No.4, red and white sewing threads, four eyelet studs, and an eyelet punch or pliers.

Cut out the main piece, 52cm x 81cm, and the circular base, 28cm in diameter, from main fabric. Cut two base pieces the same size, and one main piece, 44cm x 81cm, from lining.

Cut 3cm-wide bias strips from red cotton and join together to make a 90cm long strip. Fold and tack it over piping cord No.3. Join the ends to make a ring 78cm in circumference.

With wrong sides together, pin and tack the main base to one base lining piece 1.5cm from the edge. Clip the seam allowances of the piping, and with raw edges matching, place it on the main fabric side of the base and tack along the previous tacking line. Machine stitch close to the piping cord.

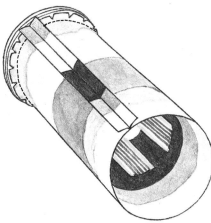

Turn under 1.5cm of the main piece to the wrong side along each short edge and press. With right sides together and starting at one fold line, pin and tack the lower edge of the main piece to the base along the stitching line. Clip into the seam allowances of the main piece to ease fabric round the circle and machine stitch in place. Pin, tack and stitch the side seam. Make up the lining in the same way.

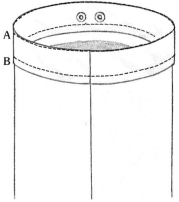

Turn 5mm to the wrong side along the top edge; pin, tack and stitch. Turn over a further 4.5cm and stitch close to the top edge A. Attach eyelet studs to the right side of the bag, one at each side of the seam and two directly opposite these.

Insert lining into the bag, slip the top edge under the turning and stitch close to edge B.

Cut piping cord No.4 in half. Using a bodkin and starting at one side of the seam, thread one length of cord all round the bag to the other side of the seam. Knot the ends together. Repeat from the other side of the bag with the second length to complete drawstring.

Umbrella carrier

A canvas carrier is the neat and easy way to take an assortment of umbrellas for the family when the weather looks doubtful.

You will need: 75cm x 40cm of canvas, two D-rings, 1.10m of webbing or strong tape to fit D-rings and matching sewing thread.

Trim 5cm from length of canvas to give a piece 75cm x 40cm. Fold in half lengthwise with wrong sides together to make a fold line.

Cut a 10cm length of webbing and thread it on two D-rings. Place the raw ends of webbing together, fold under 2cm and pin to canvas, on the fold line, 10cm from raw edge. Stitch in place close to the edges of the webbing, then reinforce with two diagonal rows of stitching. This will be the top of the carrier.

Attach remaining webbing to canvas, on the fold line, 8cm from lower edge, folding under 2cm and stitching in place as before. Neaten remaining raw edge by turning under a 2cm double hem and machine stitching in the same way, with matching thread.

Fold canvas right sides together with selvedges level, and stitch along the length, 16cm from the fold. Stitch across the lower edge to the fold. Fasten off securely. Do not trim threads too close to seam.

Make a base for the carrier by refolding the lower edge so that the side seam and the fold line on the opposite edge lie directly under the bottom seam. Press flat and stitch across the corners 4cm from each end of the bottom seam, checking that seams still match.

At top end of carrier turn 5mm then 3cm to wrong side. Stitch close to inner folded edge.

Turn carrier through to right side. Attach tape to double D-ring by slotting the end through both rings and then bringing it back through the space between the rings. Adjust to required length.

Knitted purse

Slipstitch produces a firm fabric with a neat strong edge, just right for a little evening purse decorated with shiny sequins and beads.

You will need: one 50g ball of bouclé double knitting, a pair of 4mm needles, a bag frame, sequins and beads, and matching sewing thread.

Tension
The tension for this bag was 8 sts and 8 rows to 4cm over patt, but this might vary according to the yarn used, so make a tension square and work out how wide your frame must be before purchasing it.

Cast on 24 sts. K 1 row. Tighten the first stitch at the beginning of every row as the bobbles on bouclé yarn tend to catch back a small amount of yarn and leave an uneven stitch.

Next row and every foll row: Sl 1, K to end.
Cont working in this way until 45 rows are completed. Cast off loosely.

Fold knitting in half. Backstitch loosely 7cm up each side, about 5mm in from the edge. Using scissor points, gently ease the two top edges of the knitting into the groove of the bag frame. Secure with slip stitches.

Sew beads and sequins in a line along the fold, add sequins to the front.

Slipping stitches: knitwise

Insert point of right-hand needle through the next stitch on the left-hand needle, from the front of the loop through to the back. Leave yarn at back of the work.

Without wrapping yarn around the needle, slip the stitch off the left-hand needle on to the right-hand needle. Hold yarn gently at back of work. Keep yarn at back of work if next stitch is a knit stitch.

Slipping stitches: purlwise

Insert point of right-hand needle through next stitch on left-hand needle from front of loop.

Slip stitch on to right-hand needle, holding yarn gently in front of the work. If next stitch is to be purled, keep yarn at the front.

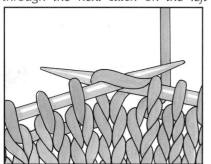

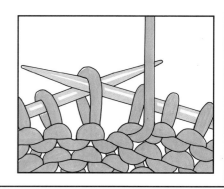

Victorian beaded purse & variations

Exquisitely knitted purses just large enough to hold essentials and thickly encrusted with beads in glowing coloured patterns are as useful and as chic now as they were in their Victorian and Edwardian heyday.

You will need: six 10m reels of Gütermann silk buttonhole thread in main yarn colour (A); three 10m reels in first yarn contrast colour (B); one 10m reel in second yarn contrast colour (C); 2000 beads, 2mm in diameter, in main bead colour (D); 550 beads, 2mm in diameter in con-

trast colour (E); 400 beads in each of three contrast colours (F, G, H); 600 beads in each of two contrast colours (I, J); 200 beads in contrast colour (K), and a set of four 2mm and 1½mm needles pointed at both ends.

Tension

42sts and 50 rows to 10cm over bead patt on 1½mm needles.

Special note: Beads must be threaded on to yarn in colour A before work is begun. Thread each reel with enough beads to complete that reel as folls:
1st reel – beads for 1st-6th rows
2nd reel – beads for 7th-17th rows
3rd reel – beads for 18th-28th rows
4th reel – beads for 29th-39th rows
5th reel – beads for 40th-46th rows
Thread the beads in reverse order to the order in which they are knitted, reading each row on the threading chart from left to right. For example, thread beads on to the 1st reel as foll:
Begin at left-hand side of 6th row of chart, thread 3 beads in F, 3 beads in G, 3 beads in D; repeat this sequence 10 times. Now begin at left-hand side

of 5th row and thread beads for that row as shown on chart. Continue threading beads for 4th, 3rd, 2nd then 1st row.
The first reel is now threaded.
If possible, buy beads on strings and transfer them to the yarn over a slip knot. If they are loose, pick them up with a beading needle on to a cotton thread and again transfer them over a slip knot.

Using four 1½mm needles and 1st reel in A threaded with beads for 1st-6th rounds, cast on 90 sts. Work in rounds.
Knit 2 rounds without placing beads.

Commence bead patt.
Next round (K1 tbl drawing next bead through stitch as shown in Placing the beads) to end. This round forms the patt.
Rep this round until 6th round is complete.
Thread beads for 7th-17th rounds on to 2nd reel in A beg with 17th round and reading each row on chart from left to right.

Work in patt until 17th round is complete.
Thread beads for 18th-28th rounds on to 3rd reel in A, beg with 28th round.
Work in patt until 28th round is complete.
Thread beads for 29th-39th rounds on to 4th reel in A, beg with 39th round.
Work in patt until 39th round is complete.
Thread beads for 40th-46th rounds on to 5th reel in A, beg with 46th round.
Work in patt until 46th round is complete.
Change to 2mm needles.
Next round With A, K tbl to end.
Next round K to end.
Rep last round twice.
Change to B and cont in st st (every round K) for 8 rounds.
Change to A. Cont in st st for 4 rounds.
Next round K2, *yfwd, K2 tog, K3, rep from * ending last repeat K1 instead of K3.
Next round K to end.
Next round P to end.
Rep last 2 rounds once more.
Change to C. Cast off loosely.

Bead threading chart

Foldline

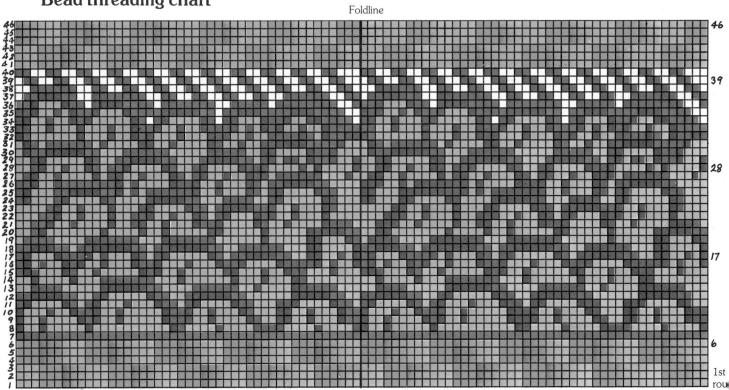

■ · ■ D ■ E ■ F ■ G □ H ■ I ■ J □ K

Note: When threading beads read each row on the chart from left to right. When knitting, read each row from right to left.

Turn work inside out. Fold bag flat along foldline marked on threading chart. Join bottom of bag with a backstitch seam. Finger press flat and turn right side out.

Using B, make 2 twisted cords approx 64cm long, using 4 strands of silk for each one. Knot each cord approx 15cm from both ends.

Thread cords through eyelet holes in top of purse so that ends of one cord are at one side and ends of other cord are at opposite side.

Thread beads on to unravelled strands at ends of each cord to make tassels.

Knot strands to secure beads. Knot ends of cords together about 3cm from tassels.

Adapting the beaded purse

Use the basic pattern to make several versions of this pretty purse or change its character by using completely different beads – glittering golds and silvers or dramatic jet and crystal.

The bead threading chart on page 22 shows the whole of the beaded section of the purse. To alter the design simply copy the basic grid (90 stitches by 46 rows) on to graph paper and fill in the squares with a different motif or pattern. Remember that the purse itself is worked in rounds so that left- and right-hand sides of the chart must be matched. To make the purse larger or smaller increase or decrease the number of stitches and rows. When the new chart is complete count the number of squares in each colour to give you the necessary quantities of beads. Any existing charted pattern can be adapted for the purse providing that the repeat can be fitted into the number of cast-on stitches. If the chart shows the repeat only, extend it to cover the threading chart for the whole beaded section of the bag.

Placing the beads

1 Thread the beads on to the yarn before beginning to knit. Place the beads on every stitch of every round as follows. Hold the yarn with the beads in your left hand. Insert the right-hand needle knitwise into the first stitch of the round through the back of the loop.

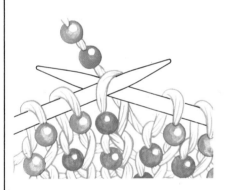

2 Use the right-hand needle to open the stitch. Use the left middle finger to slide the next bead up close to the stitch and push it from behind into the loop ready to be pulled through to the right side.

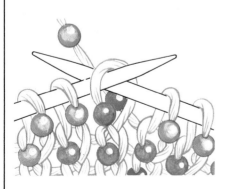

3 To complete the stitch, hook the tip of the right-hand needle behind the yarn and draw it through the loop while bringing the bead through at the same time.

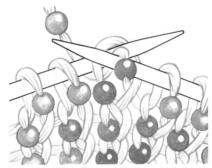

Stocking stitch

Since the purse is worked in the round, all the beading is done on knit rows, but if you wish to knit a stocking stitch design you should, on purl rows, purl the first stitch through the back of the loop. Purl the next stitch through the back of the loop, pushing the bead through the stitch to the back of the work as the yarn is pulled through. Beads are placed on every stitch in the row except the first and the last ones.

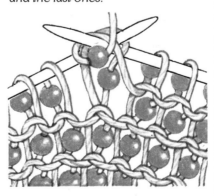

Charting motifs for purse beading

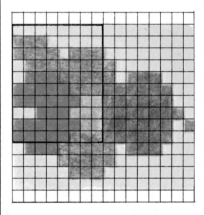

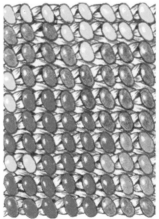

Should you wish to work your own design, chart your chosen motifs on graph paper as shown, allowing one square for each stitch/bead. Thread the beads starting at the top of the chart, reading the even-numbered rows from right to left and the odd-numbered rows from left to right. The bead in the bottom right-hand corner will be the last to be threaded.

Sample patterns

Beaded purses make lovely gifts for friends or relatives, so experiment with these patterns, or create your own colourful designs.

1 **Sun spots**
Simple geometric shapes like these circles can very easily be reproduced in purse beading. This sample is worked with beads in five different colours.

2 **Beaded checks**
The squares in the checks are filled in with a range of diagonal, horizontal and vertical strips making what is ultimately a rather intricate pattern with beads in seven colours.

3 **Terrazzo**
This sample is worked in five colours. It is based on an old traditional tile pattern and repeats over 7 stitches and 10 rows.

4

4 Beaded chevron
Beads in six colours are used in this sample. The pattern repeats over 10 stitches and could be adapted for the basic purse.

2

5

5 Bead borders
The lines of yellow beads separate three different border patterns. The lower two could both be adapted for the basic purse.

Appliqué bag

Make this pretty silk evening bag with a delicate appliqué motif in colours to match your favourite party outfit.

You will need: two pieces of silk, with light-weight wadding and lining, 18cm x 16.5cm, 10cm x 10cm of purple silk, small strip of silver lamé, paper-backed bonding, 15cm zip, 1.50m of narrow silver cord, 8 small glass beads, matching sewing threads.

Transfer the motif to the paper side of the bonding and cut out each shape separately. Iron the pieces on to silver lamé and purple silk as indicated and

cut out. With 18cm forming width of silk, position the pieces at the centre. Press to fix them in place.

With right side up, tack silk front to lining, with wadding in between. Machine round the edges of the motif in matching threads, using a small zigzag stitch. Machine lines of fan with tiny straight stitch, and trailing cord with tiny zigzag stitch. Sew beads in place on scalloped edge.

Zigzag stitch through all layers along top edge to neaten. Turn 1cm to the wrong side and tack in place. Prepare the back of the bag in the same way.

Pin bag front and back to zip, placing top folded edges next to zip teeth. Tack securely, then stitch using a zipper foot attachment.

Open zip, fold bag right sides together and stitch round three sides, 1.5cm from edge. Neaten seam with small machine zigzag stitch close to stitching. Trim excess fabric and turn the bag through.

Thread a large darning needle with silver cord and knot the end. Bring the cord out at one end of the zip and thread it back into the bag at the other. Knot securely.

Drawstring bag

This pretty bag with its matching scarf is so quick and easy to sew that you can make several, changing the colours and textures so that you have one for each outfit in your wardrobe.

You will need: 1m of 90cm-wide fabric, machine sewing thread, 2m of fine gold shirring elastic, 60cm of gold piping, 11cm x 11cm of interfacing,

2m of matching cord and three decorative gold leaves.

Cut two pieces of fabric 58cm x 23cm. Mark lines for shirring across 58cm width of one piece, on right side. Mark two lines for the casing, 5cm and 6.5cm from the top, and three more 3cm apart.

Fold each piece of fabric in half, right sides together, and stitch side seams along 23cm length, leaving a 1.5cm space on unmarked piece 5cm from top for the drawstring.

Place the piece with the partly stitched seam inside the other, right sides together. Pin and tack piping between the two, 1.5cm from top edge. Machine through all three layers. Turn right side out and press.

With marked side right side up, tack two layers together between shirring lines and shir using the machine method, with shirring elastic on the bobbin. Make small pleats along bottom edge, so that it measures 35cm.

Cut two circles of fabric and one circle of interfacing 11cm in diameter. Place interfacing between pieces of fabric. Pin and machine to pleated edge, right sides together, to make the base. Trim and neaten edges.

Turn bag right side out. Cut a Length of cord 140cm. Sew each end inside the bag on opposite sides. Insert remaining cord for drawstring. Knot ends. Attach leaves.

Cut piece of fabric 1m x 25cm for scarf and roll a tiny hem on all four edges. Machine stitch hem.

27

Quilted shoulder bag

If you enjoy quilting, display your skill with this pretty shoulder bag, stitched in delicate colours.

You will need: 30cm x 60cm each of silk, lining fabric and polyester wadding; two reels each of thread, one a shade darker than the silk fabric and a contrasting colour; 2.5m of a silky cord trim; a sheet of tracing paper; dressmaker's carbon paper; a sharp pencil or tracing wheel, and a small tapestry frame for quilting, if desired.

Cut a 2.5cm strip from one end of the silk fabric and place on one side. Fold the remaining silk in half lengthwise.

Draw up the purse shapes from the graph in which one square equals two centimetres and transfer to the silk fabric. Trace off the two quilting designs and pin to the wrong side of the carbon paper. Using a tracing wheel or sharp pencil, transfer the design to the pattern pieces as indicated.

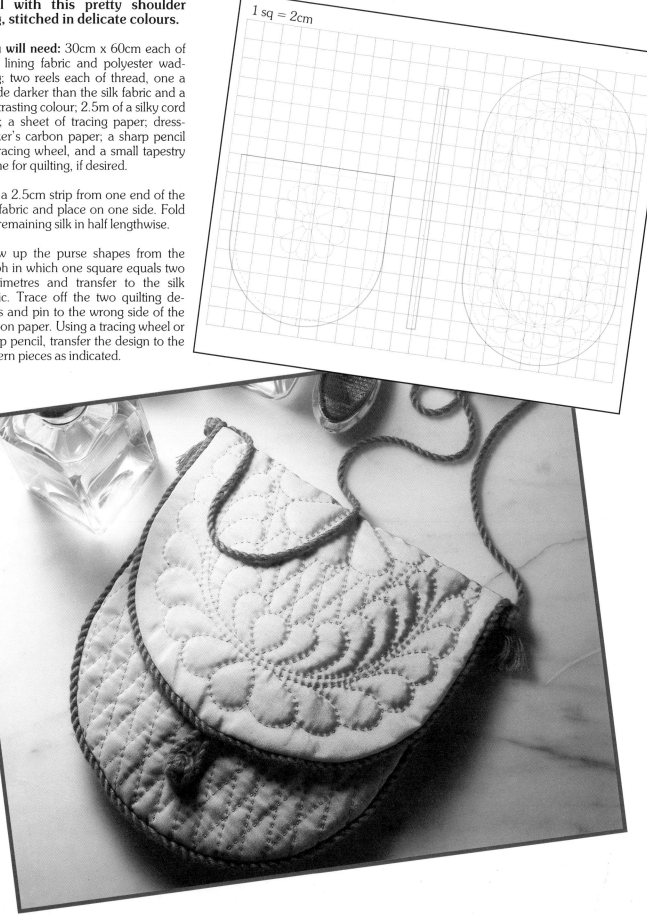

1 sq = 2cm

To draw the diagonal lines for the background quilting, place pattern piece C as a continuation of the centre lines of the flower shape (see arrows to indicated where to begin). Use C to draw in the rest of the quilting lines, continuing the diagonal pattern to the edges of the feathers on pattern piece A, to the extreme edges of piece B.

Sandwich the wadding between the lining and the top fabric. Pin and tack the fabrics together all round. Place in the frame for quilting if desired, making sure all layers are evenly stretched.

Taking approximately nine stitches to every 2.5cm, quilt the background in the darker thread, the flowers and feathers in the contrast colour. Remove the work from the frame.

Cut out the purse shapes. Bind the top edge of piece B with the 2.5cm fabric strip. Trim wadding between fabrics. Turn in and slipstitch the seam allowances around the purse flap.

Slip the seam allowances of piece B between those of piece A around the base of purse and slipstitch into place. Turn the purse right side out and slipstitch silky cord around the edges.

Make a loop from cord and sew to the centre front of the purse flap. Make a Chinese knot and sew it to the front of the purse as a button to match loop. Tie a knot at each end of the remaining cord. Trim the ends to about 1.5cm and fray them to make small tassels. Sew the cord handle to the purse, as shown.

Making a Chinese knot

Cut a strip of fabric 2.5cm wide and 20cm long. Fold in half lengthwise, with right sides together. Machine, leaving a 6mm seam. Trim the seam

close to the stitching. Turn the rouleau strip to the right side, using a bodkin or blunt knitting needle.

To tie the knot, start at point A. Make two loops, one on top of the other. Thread the other end of the rouleau strip alternatively over and under the

loops to end at point B. Pull gently to tighten the knot. Trim the ends and stitch together, then slipstitch the knot on to the bag.

Chapter 2
B·E·L·T·S & B·R·A·C·E·S

A belt will draw attention to the waist, add
colour or texture to a plain dress or combination
of separates, gather in fullness or give some
measure of support to a garment. Usually their
design and width are either dictated by fashion
or the shape of the body (wide belts tend not to
suit the short waisted).

If you have never worked in leather before, belt
making is a good way to start – you will find it a
lot easier than you imagined. Alternatively,
experiment with some of the sewn or knitted
belts shown here, choosing colours to co-
ordinate your outfits and chime with your shoes.

Each square ≡ 2cm

Buckle position
Enlarge or reduce here

FRONT
Cut 2

SIDE
SECTION
Cut 4

Slit

Enlarge or reduce here

Wide fashion belt

Wear this stylish belt outside a classic Aran or chunky jumper for a fashionable finish to a winter outfit.

You will need: a real or imitation leather skin approximately 55cm x 55cm or large enough for pattern pieces (the leather for the under piece need not be perfect), a kilt buckle in a contrast colour, thread to match leather, thread and buttonhole twist to match buckle, and a large or leather point machine needle.

Scale up the pattern pieces from the grid to make the belt for average 67cm waist. For a tighter fit or a smaller waist, reduce the pattern by subtracting half the required amount from side front at position indicated and redraw-

ing a smooth edge. Enlarge by adding half the required amount in same way.

Cut out two front and four side section pieces in leather, placing the side section pattern piece wrong side up for two of the four pieces, to make two right and two left side section pieces.

Join front to sides by overlapping edges by 5mm and machining a straight-stitched seam in matching thread. Zigzag stitch raw edges of overlap on right side to neaten. Repeat for remaining front and side sections to form under piece.

Lay two belt pieces wrong sides together. Wind contrast buttonhole twist on to bobbin by hand and thread the contrast sewing thread on the top.

Loosen bobbin tension slightly and test stitch on a spare piece of leather. With under piece uppermost, topstitch around belt 5mm from the edge to give bold stitching line on the right side of the belt.

Make a slit on the left-side section at the position indicated on the pattern. Zigzag stitch edges in matching thread to neaten.

Try on the belt, threading right-hand end of belt through slit. The belt should fit snugly round a normal waistline with ends meeting. Trim ends to eliminate any overlap.

Machine stitch the kilt buckle to each end of the belt, using matching thread and a regular straight stitch.

Appliqué belt

This stunning cummerbund tie belt in suede and leather has a contrast centre section decorated with appliqué triangles.

You will need: approximately 45cm x 15cm of leather for the centre panel, approximately 60cm x 30cm of contrast suede for end sections and triangles, thread to match centre section, and suede adhesive.

Scale up the pattern pieces from the grid to make a belt for a 67cm to 76cm waist (1.5cm seam allowances are included). Cut out one centre section from leather and two end sections from suede. From remaining suede, cut 7 triangles in different sizes varying between 3.5cm and 5.5cm along the edges.

Arrange triangles randomly on the right side of the centre section, all within 2.5cm from the outer edges. Glue them in place. When dry, stitch around the edges of the triangles with a close zigzag stitch.

Fold and glue 1.5cm to wrong side around pointed ends of centre section. Overlap pointed ends of centre section over corresponding ends of each end section. Glue in place, then topstitch near to folded edge of centre section.

Make 1cm snips around the curved ends of the belt. Fold and glue 1.5cm to the wrong side around the outer edges. Flatten bulky sections by tapping with a suede-covered hammer. Topstitch 1cm in from the outer edge of the belt.

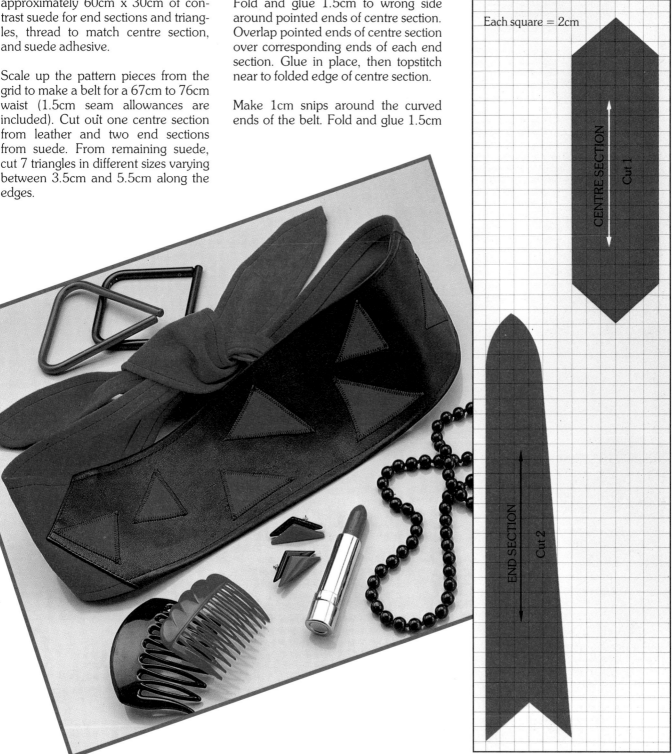

Each square = 2cm

CENTRE SECTION Cut 1

END SECTION Cut 2

Sporty belt

Even an inexperienced knitter could easily make this attractive casual belt in cotton – perfect with summer co-ordinates.

You will need: one 50g ball of Twilley's cotton, 2¾mm needles and a buckle.

Tension
11 sts measures 3½cm wide to fit the

buckle shown. Choose your own buckle before starting to knit the belt, preferably selecting a clip-shut type without a prong, which will not wear your knitting. When you have chosen the buckle, make a tension sample and place it through the fastener. Make adjustments, if necessary, keeping an uneven number of stitches.

Using 2¾mm needles, cast on 11 sts

and work patt as follows:
1st row: K1 * P1, K1, rep from * to end.
2nd row: K1 * P1, K1, rep from * to end.
These 2 rows form the patt. Work on these sts until work meas 110cm from beg, cast off.

Finish by sewing the cast-off end to the buckle neatly on the wrong side.

Trimmed tie belt

Another easy-knit belt for summer wear, this time decorated with beaded tassels and cords. Wear it to add interest to a plain dress or to make a blouson effect with a full one.

You will need: one 50g ball of dish-cloth cotton in main colour (A), one 50g ball each of contrast colours (B and C), approximately 100 small beads and a pair of 4mm needles.

Tension
20 sts and 24 rows to 10cm over patt on 4mm needles.

Using 4mm needles and A, cast on 26sts. Work in st st for 7 rows.
Using B, work 2 rows of st st. Using A, work 12 rows in st st. Rep from * to * 5 times.
Using B, work 2 rows in st st.
Using A, work 6 rows in st st.
Cast off.

Cut 4 strands of B, 14cm long; thread through darning needle. Starting from the left of belt between 1st and 2nd ridge of B, count up 9 rows and 13 sts from 1st ridge. Pass strands through st leaving an equal amount on each side. Tie a knot in the centre so 8 strands hang from knot. Sew a bead on each end.
Rep making tassel with 3 strands on the next ridge, foll with next tassel with 8 strands. Rep to end of belt.

Fold belt in half lengthwise and join seam. With right sides facing and C, pick up sts from cast-on edge. (12 sts.)
Next row: P.
Work 4 rows in st st.
Dec 1 st at beg of next 8 rows. (4 sts.)
Cast off.
Sew on beads in rows on each of the triangles.

To make a large tassel: cut 3 lengths of C, 144cm long. Fold each in half and knot at folded end. Divide into three and plait. Thread on beads at random. When plait is completed, knot end.
Thread a bead at each end. Repeat to make the second large tassel. Sew on to cast-off edges of belt.

Lacy suede belt

Turn a blouse and skirt into a cocktail outfit with this hole-punched and gathered suede frill.

You will need: approximately 25cm x 75cm of real or imitation suede, matching thread, a multi-sized hole punch, and pinking shears.

Cut two 3cm-wide strips of suede, equal to your waist measurement plus 1cm all round for seams, two 6cm-wide frill strips twice this length, and eight 50mm x 50cm strips for the ties of the belt.

Turn under and press 1cm around all edges of both centre strips and turn and stitch the short edges of each frill strip.

Following the diagram opposite and using a multi-sized hole punch work a zigzag border 1.5cm from the top edge of each frill strip. (Note: placing a piece of card behind the fabric makes it easier to punch the holes.)

Using pinking shears, cut the top edge of each frill strip, gather the opposite

edges and pull up to fit the centre strips. Sandwich the frills and the ties between the two centre strips and topstitch neatly all round.

Wear the belt with ties knotted at the centre front, back or at one side.

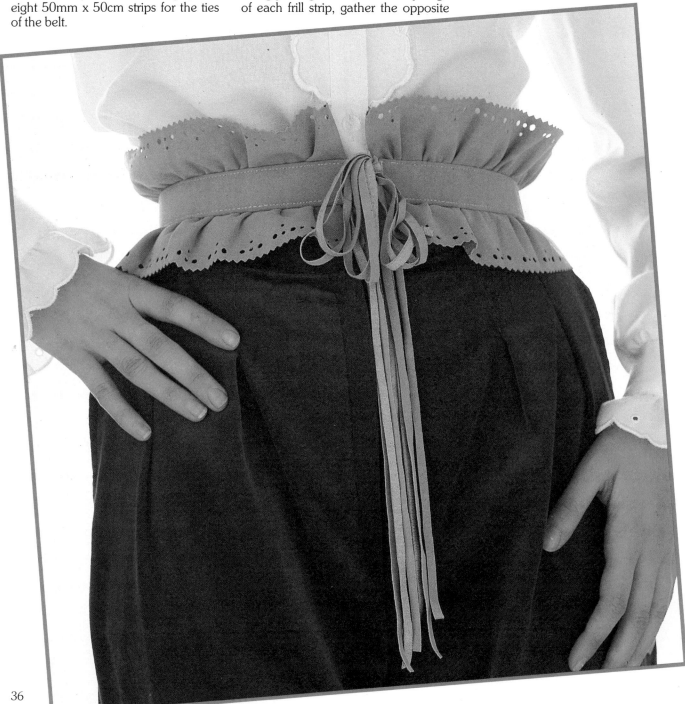

Braided belt

Nothing could be simpler to make than this colourful, kaleidoscopic belt of twisted, beaded and whipped braids.

You will need: 1.5m lengths of about 10 assorted braids, 3m each of three colours of Russia braid, assorted large beads.

Thread individual strands of braid with beads, as desired, and knot the ends.

Holding the cords at both ends, twist tightly and tape to a flat surface.

Whip around the twisted braids with approximately 50cm lengths of Russia braid to hold them snugly round the waist. Use remaining Russia braid on the loose ends.

Twist the belt again for wearing.

Flowery belt

Simple padded flowers turn a length of brightly-coloured cord into a stunning belt.

You will need: 2m length of multi-coloured cord, 20cm x 30cm of patterned cotton fabric, 6cm x 26cm of 56g (2oz) wadding, oddments of wool and scraps of suede.

Knot the ends of cord, fold it in half and mark the centre point. Cut six pieces of fabric, each 6.5cm x 15cm, and six pieces of wadding, each 2cm x 13cm.

With wrong sides facing, fold each piece of fabric in half lengthways, enclosing the wadding. With the fold at the top, round off the top corners. Using double thread, work a row of running stitches along the bottom edge through both layers of fabric.

Make centre tufts by cutting the wool into 4.5cm lengths. Stitch a small group of tufts to one end of each piece of fabric.

Pull up the running thread into gathers and secure them. Roll the wadded pieces into flowers and stitch them to the centre of the cord.

Cut a 5cm circle of suede and stick it to the back of the belt to cover the underside of the flowers.

Cut out leaf shapes from remaining of suede and stitch them in place.

Multicoloured belt

Girdle yourself with a canvas-work kaleidoscope of pattern and colour.

You will need: a strip of canvas with 18 holes to 2.5cm, 10cm wide by the length of your waist measurement, plus turnings; a piece of lining fabric to match; one skein each of perlé embroidery thread in colours of your choice; lining fabric; matching thread, and a suitable buckle.

Leaving an equal border at either side of the canvas, divide it into blocks measuring 12 holes by 12 holes.

Using the photograph as a guide, fill in each small square with patterns in the colours and stitches of your choice. The stitches used in the belt shown are ringed square, tent, Rhodes, eyelet, mosaic, Gobelin, cross, double cross, jacquard, cushion, chessboard filling, chequer, Norwich and satin stitch.

Turn and press the border canvas to the wrong side of the belt; repeat for the belt lining.

Slipstitch the lining to the wrong side of the belt.

Turn in and slipstitch each end of the belt. Finish off by attaching the prettiest buckle you can find.

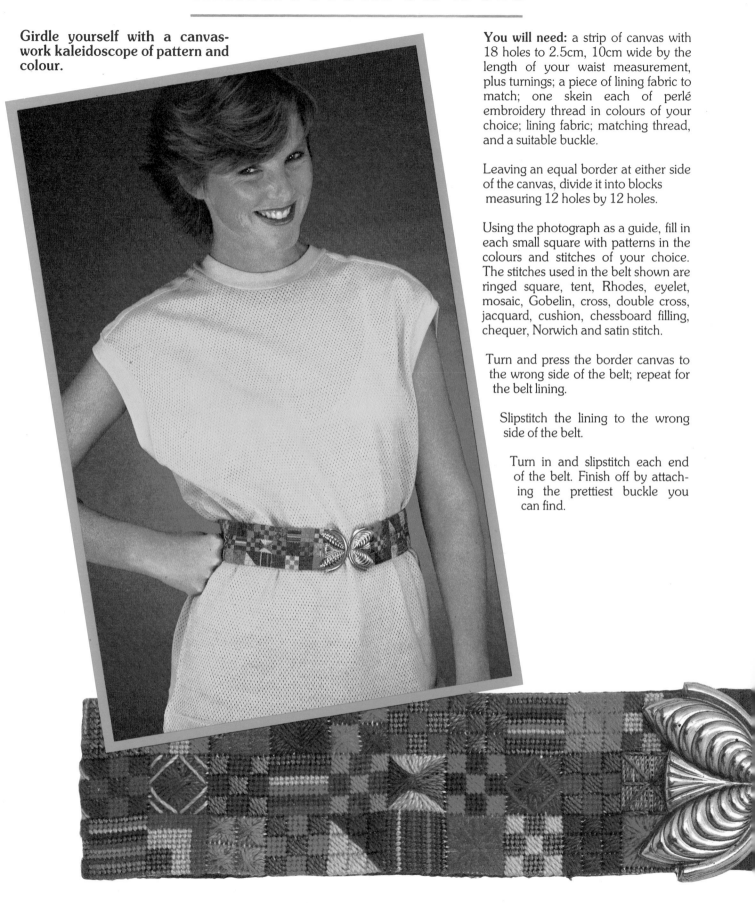

Tyrolean belt & shoe rosettes

Clinch the waist of a very full dress or draw attention to a peasant-style skirt with this attractive front-lacing belt. Make shoe rosettes to match.

You will need: two pieces of 9cm-wide fabric and one piece of heavyweight, non-woven interfacing equal to your waist measurement plus 1cm all round for turnings; 1m of matching cord to tie; matching thread and an eyelet punch.

The belt
With the belt fabrics right sides facing, interfacing on top, and leaving a gap for turning, machine round all edges of the belt curving all corners. Turn right side out and press under a damp cloth, then slipstitch the opening. Slipstitch approximately 1.60m of cord around the edges of the belt.

Using an eyelet punch, make three holes at each end of the belt approximately 1.5cm from the raw edges.

Thread the holes with a 1m length of cord and tie up to fit.

Shoe rosettes
Cut two 12.5cm x 16cm pieces of fabric. Leaving a gap for turning, fold each piece in half along the length and stitch all edges. Turn strips right side out and press. Fold and stitch ends to middles and gather the centre of each loop to form a bow. Trim with bows made out of cord. Glue each rosette to an old earring and clip in place.

Leather cummerbund

This eye-catching cummerbund is made from soft kid with a metallic sheen and embellished with gold thread work and leather appliqué.

You will need: one small leather skin (preferably kid) at least 71cm in one direction, 15cm x 7.5cm of gold kid, one skein of Elizabethan gold twist, one strand of fine pearl purl, one strand of fine smooth purl, beeswax to make the threads run smoothly, fine silk thread in matching colour, size 7 and size 9 crewel needles, one beading needle, an eyelet punch, and a buckle at least 2.5cm wide.

Enlarge the pattern for the belt and mark out the correct size on the back of the skin. Remember to mark out two, as one is used to back the belt. Matching the centre front of the belt and using this as the centre of the design, transfer the goldwork design on to the back of the leather.

Ruche the centre of the gold kid and secure with a few tiny stitches. Cut out the centre design and position it on the belt; stitch neatly in place. While doing this, keep the kid taut in an embroidery hoop, taking care not to pull it so tightly as to stretch the leather. Remove leather from the hoop when the appliqué is complete.

Couch down a double length of Elizabethan twist all round the edge of the appliqué to neaten and define the edge. Using a single strand of the same thread, couch down the 'webbing' of the design. Finally apply the pearl purl and smooth purl by laying short lengths at various angles at the centre of the ruched gold kid.

Cut out both pieces of leather to the pattern shape, cutting the backing leather to the exact size and allowing 1cm turning all round the front piece. Place the two pieces together, right sides outwards, and fold the turning over to the back: cut the corners diagonally to avoid bulk. Stitch in place.

Cut out the tabs for the buckle. Place two of them together, right sides outwards, and stitch together by machining 2mm from the edge. Punch four holes in this tab. Attach the buckle to the other tab and machine stitch both tabs in place on the belt.

Goldwork belt

A stunning belt to wear with icy summer whites, this is bound to prove a gilt-edged investment for your wardrobe.

You will need: 1m x 20cm of calico fabric, 91cm x 25cm of cream silk, 91cm x 10cm of non-woven interfacing and lining fabric, a selection of gold and bronze coloured beads, braids and threads, and a suitable fastening.

Ideally, you should work the embroidery in a slate frame. Tack the silk to the calico and mount it in the frame. Draw up the pattern from the graph and using dressmaker's carbon paper, transfer the design to the silk fabric. Using fine wool, tack around the outline of the design. Working from the centre of the design and using the photograph for reference, stitch the beads in place and couch pieces of gold thread and braid along the marked lines.

Press the work from the wrong side and remove from the frame. Cut interfacing to shape and tack to the wrong side of the fabric.

Trim the seam allowance of the belt and lining fabric to 1.5cm. Turn and press to the wrong side.

Place the belt and the lining wrong sides together and slipstitch round all the edges.

Stitch the fastening into place.

Fold the fabric strip across the length and place the centre of the design to the fold. Continue the straight edges for a further 20cms.

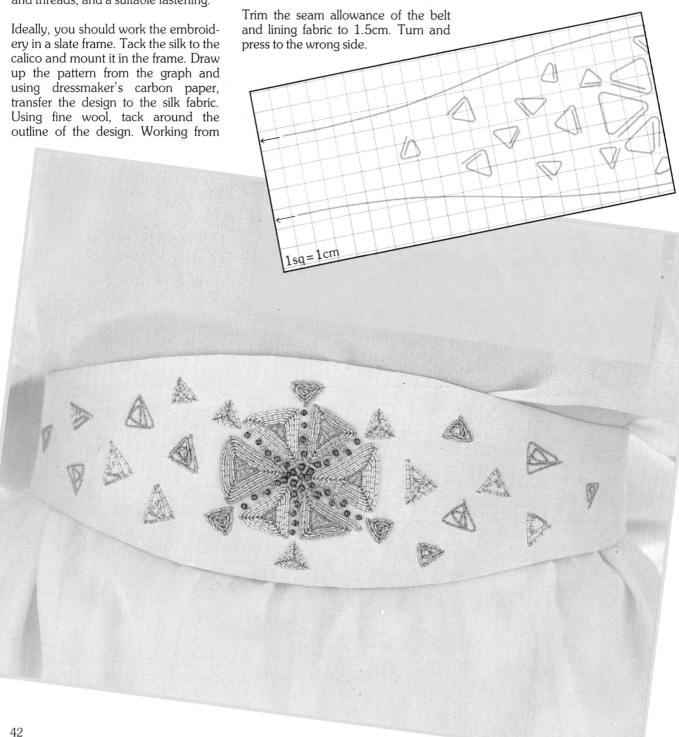

1sq=1cm

Cord belt

This unusual belt made in matching cords and cotton fabric looks good with a summer skirt or trousers. Choose plain colours for the best effect.

You will need: 10cm of 90cm-wide medium-weight cotton (for a belt to fit 66cm-76cm waist), 4m of cord in main colour, 3m of cord in second colour, 4cm buckle, paper-backed bonding, hole punching kit and six coloured eyelets, and fabric adhesive.

Trace the diamond shape from the page and add a 6mm seam allowance all round to make the paper template. Cut six diamond shapes in cotton and press seam allowances to wrong.

Trim the seam allowance from the template, cutting just inside the original line. Cut three shapes in cotton and three in paper-backed bonding. Apply bonding shapes to cotton shapes, following the manufacturer's instructions. Remove paper and apply to the wrong side of three of the six prepared shapes. These faced diamonds are used on the right side of the belt.

Make the template for buckle end of belt by cutting the paper template in half along the dotted line AB and arranging resulting triangles on paper so that the distance between points C and D is 13cm. Join triangles at top and bottom to make a long hexagon. Add 6mm all round and cut out. Cut two shapes in cotton and turn seam allowances to the wrong side. Trim seam allowances from template: cut one in cotton and one in paper-backed bonding. Face one shape as for the diamonds and bond to the second shape.

Make a template for the overlap end of the belt in the same way, spacing triangles 23cm apart. Cut two in cotton and turn seam allowances to the wrong side. Trim seam allowance from template and cut one in cotton and one in paper-backed bonding. Face one prepared shape as before.

Lay three unfaced diamond shapes wrong side up with 16cm between

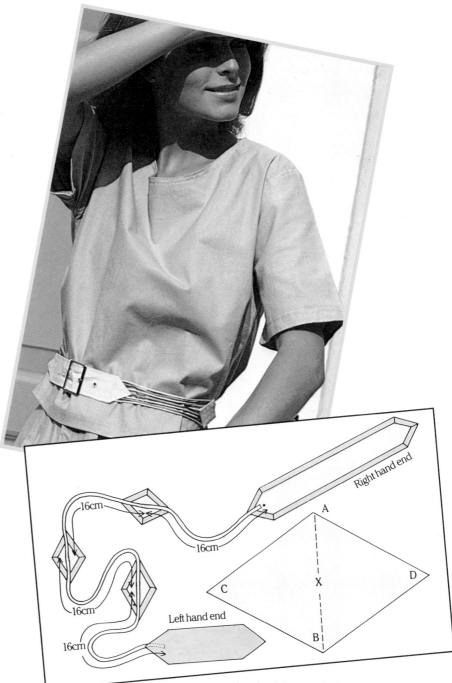

centre points X. Place unfaced overlap end wrong side up at right-hand side, and buckle end at left-hand side faced side down, with 16cm between centre points of diamonds as before.

Lay cords from centre of the diamond at overlap end to centre of diamond at buckle end, over the diamonds, arranging colours in sequence, starting and finishing with main colour. Secure to fabric pieces with fabric adhesive.

Apply fabric adhesive to the wrong side of edges of faced overlap end of belt and faced diamonds and stick to matching pieces wrong sides together.

Following the manufacturer's instructions, make eyelet at centre of faced side of buckle piece, and thread on buckle. Fold fabric to unfaced side and stick. On overlap end of belt make five eyelets at 2.5cm intervals, starting 5.5cm in from pointed end. Centre eyelet should fit waist measurement.

Patchwork belt

This striking patchwork belt is made with a form of machine patchwork invented by the Seminole Indians and used to make highly decorative bands for their clothing.

You will need: small amounts of 115cm-wide medium-weight dress cotton in each of four colours (for a belt measuring 75cm x 7cm), a strip of woven interfacing and matching sewing thread.

From the three coloured fabrics chosen for the patchwork, cut five strips the width of the fabric by 3cm. See Making the patchwork, step 1. Trim off the selvedges, press well and arrange on a board in the order in which you wish the fabrics to appear in the work.

Place the bottom two strips with right sides facing and, taking a 5mm seam, join along one long edge. Working in this way, join all strips to form one piece of fabric. When all five strips have been joined, working from the wrong side of fabric, press all seam allowances in one direction.

Place the fabric with the strips running horizontally and cut into 3cm-wide vertical strips. Take care to measure and cut these strips accurately and at right angles to the seams.

To create the diagonal pattern, arrange each strip one block further along than the one below it. See Making the patchwork, steps 4 and 5. Machine the strips together, right sides facing and taking 5mm seams. Press all seams in one direction as before. To increase the overall 'usable' length of patchwork, cut the finished strip in the centre and join the two diagonal ends together with right sides facing, taking a 5mm seam.

Make a simple clutch bag and decorate the front flap with bands of Seminole patchwork. Work in the same way as for the belt, but using three times as many strips of fabric. Line the bag with light wadding and one of the patchwork fabrics.

Trim the excess points from the top and bottom of the patchwork strip. Cut a piece of interfacing to fit the patchwork and tack to the wrong side. Cut a piece of backing fabric, 2cm larger all round than the patchwork. With wrong sides facing, place the patchwork strip in the centre of the backing fabric and machine stitch together all round through all thicknesses of fabric close to the raw edge. Turn under a small seam allowance, fold to right side and, using matching thread, slipstitch the remainder of the backing fabric neatly to the front of the patchwork.

Make two ties from left-over fabric and stitch centrally to the underside of each end of the belt.

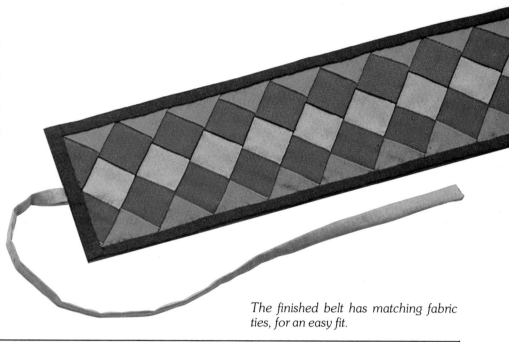

The finished belt has matching fabric ties, for an easy fit.

Making the patchwork

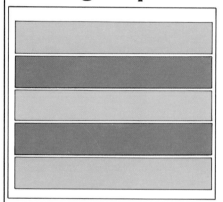

1 Seminole patchwork reduces the fabric to considerably less than its original size, so cut strips up to twice the required length and width and arrange them in the order they are to be joined.

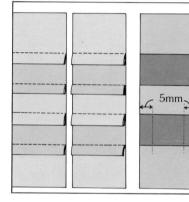

3 *Leaving seam allowances as required (the depth of each horizontal strip plus 5mm at either side), cut the joined fabrics into vertical strips. Take care to measure and cut each strip accurately.*

5 *To increase the usable length of the patchwork, cut the strip in the centre neatly along the seam and join the two diagonal ends with right sides facing, taking a 5mm seam, as before.*

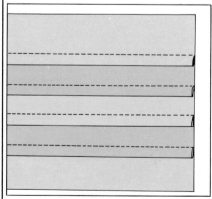

2 *Working upwards from the bottom, join the fabrics along their long edges with right sides facing and taking 5mm seams. Press seam allowances in one direction for easier stitching.*

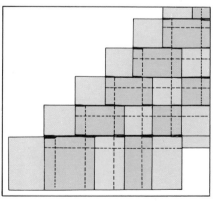

4 *Moving each strip along one block and working from the lowest strip, join the fabric strips with right sides facing carefully aligning the pattern, and taking 5mm seams. Press seam allowances in one direction.*

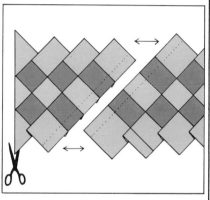

Alternative ideas for this type of patchwork include using centred motifs from printed fabrics contrasted with bright, plain colours, or, motifs could be embroidered within the patches.

White leather belt

A white leather belt, decorated with delicate cut-work embroidery, makes the perfect complement to soft, feminine summer fashions.

You will need: a piece of white medium-weight, clothing leather, 15cm x your waist measurement, 1 skein of white *au ver à soie*, silk embroidery thread, a size 7 crewel needle, a thimble, a tube of all-purpose clear adhesive, a metal straight-edge, a sharp craft knife, and an empty ball-point pen.

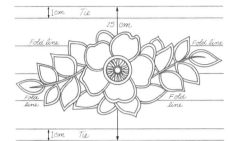

Following the diagram, mark the area of the belt on the wrong side of your

46

leather, scoring the lines with a ruler and needle. Trace off the motif and transfer it to the leather with an empty ball-point pen (pencil or dressmaker's carbon paper would soil the leather and the silk thread). Score all lines with a needle.

Using three strands of embroidery silk work French knots and buttonhole bars in the centre of the rose. To make the buttonhole bars, take the thread from the inner circle of the rose centre to the outer circle; make a small stitch and return. Take the thread back

again so that you have three threads together, then work buttonhole over these three threads. Repeat for the next bar, and continue in this way right round, then work buttonhole stitch round the inner and outer circles. When the stitching is complete, carefully cut away the leather from between the circles.

For the rest of the embroidery, use two strands of silk and work the leaves and petals in buttonhole stitch, one side of the stalks in buttonhole stitch, the other in stem stitch.

When the embroidery is complete, cut away the background leather.

Cut two 1cm-wide ties as shown and cut carefully around the top and bottom of the motif. Glue turnings to the wrong side of the belt. Glue each tie 8cm from one end of the belt. Fold in the ends to form points and cut away the excess fabric from inside the turnings. Glue the turned ends in place.

For extra strength, cut a rose motif in reverse, from leftover leather. Glue to the wrong side of the belt motif.

Trace pattern

French knots

Bring the thread out at the required position and hold it down to one side with the left thumb. Twist the thread twice round the needle, then insert it back into the fabric close to the starting point. Pull the thread through to the back, tightening the knot. Bring the needle up again for next knot.

Buttonhole stitch

Bring the needle out of the fabric by the edge of the marked line. Insert

the needle into the fabric above the line, then take a downward stitch back to just beyond the line. Loop the thread under the point of the needle and pull the needle through, tightening the loop. Repeat all round the shape.

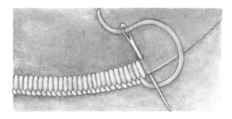

Stem stitch

1 To work a broad, twisted stem stitch, bring the needle up at the beginning of the line to be worked. Take it forward and re-insert it a little to the right of the line, keeping the thread to the right of the needle. Bring

the needle up again half way along the first stitch and slightly to the left, ready for the next stitch. Continue with even stitches to the end of the line.

2 To produce a strong, narrow line, always bring the needle up and re-insert it along the line itself.

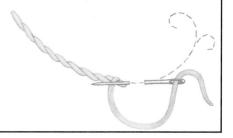

Tweedy tie & braces

Make this sporty, tweedy tie for yourself or your man in a mock rib pattern. Team it up with casual office clothes or wear it with braces for fun. For the braces, buy a pair of men's narrow braces, and sew the knitted fabric on to the elastic. The braces are worked in a cross stitch pattern, and give a sporty look.

Tweedy tie
Tension
24 sts and 38 rows to 10cm over patt on 4mm needles.

You will need: one 25g ball each of 4 ply Shetland yarn in main colour (A), and contrast colour (B), and a pair of 4mm needles.

Using A, cast on 9 sts.
1st row: *P1, sl 1 purlwise, rep from * to last st P1.
2nd row: *K1, P1 rep from * to last st, K1
3rd row: As 1st row.
4th row: As 2nd row.

5th row: Using B, work as 1st row.
6th row: Using B, work as 2nd row.
7th row: Using A, work as 1st row.
8th row: Using A, work as 2nd row.
Rep rows 5-8 inclusive until work meas 133cm from the beg, ending with a WS row.
Now work rows 1-4 inclusive using A. Cast off loosely. Darn in ends.

Braces
You will need: one 25g ball each of 4 ply Shetland yarn in main colour A, and contrast colour B, a pair of men's narrow braces and a pair of 4mm needles.

48

Measure the braces and make 4 strips the length of the longer elastic, and 2 strips the length of the shorter elastic. Using A, cast on an odd number of sts, the width required.

Work as folls:

1st row: K.

2nd row: K.

3rd row: Using B, *K1, ybk, sl 1 purlwise, rep from * to last st K1.

4th row: Using B, *K1, yfwd, sl 1 purlwise, ybk, rep from * to last st K1.

5th row: Using A, K.

6th row: Using A, K.

7th row: Using B, *ybk, sl 1 purlwise, K1 rep from * to last st, sl 1 purlwise.

8th row: Sl 1 purlwise, ybk, K1, yfwd, rep from * to last st, sl 1 purlwise.

These 8 rows form the patt, rep until the required length.

Press all the pieces carefully under a damp cloth, and darn in all the loose ends. Using a strong thread, sew the knitted pieces on to the elastic firmly and neatly.

Tubular tie

1 *Choose the yarn carefully for the tie, and knit a small sample. If the work is not very firm the tie will not lie flat. In this case it is better to work twice the width, and join a seam. This seam can then be placed at the centre back of the tie. It is necessary to work on an uneven number of stitches to keep the pattern correct.*

2 *Fold the work in half with the wrong side of the work facing. Using a darning needle, work in back stitch from the bottom end of the tie to the top. Do not stitch the cast-on and casting-off edge. Turn the work so the right side is facing. Sew the top and bottom of the tie, neatly catching one stitch from each side.*

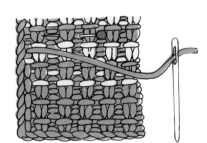

Belt & braces

If you prefer a belt and braces to a tie and braces, you can either adapt the slipstitch patterns given on the previous page or liven up your jeans with the more colourful stocking stitch patterns shown here.

For the striped bar belt and braces you will need: oddments of 4 ply yarn in main colour (A) and four contrast colours (B, C, D and E).

For the chequers belt and braces: oddments of 4 ply yarn in main colour (A) and contrast colour (B).

For both you will also need: 30cm x 30cm leather or felt (for one pair of braces), a buckle and 80cm of 3cm-wide elastic (for one belt), and one pair of 3mm knitting needles.

Tension

10 sts and 8 rows to 3.5cm over striped bar or chequers patt on 3mm knitting needles.

Braces (make 2)

With A, cast on 10 sts.
** **Next Row** K1, P1, K6, P1, K1.
Next Row P1, K1, P6, K1, P1. **

Work in either striped bar patt or chequers patt as foll:
1st row K1A, P1A, *work 1st row of patt, rep from * to last 2 sts, P1A, K1A.
2nd row P1A, K1A, *work 2nd row of patt, rep from * to last 2 sts, K1A, P1A.
These 2 rows establish the patt, with border sts.
Keeping patt correct cont until work measures 72cm, ending with a WS row.
Cont in A only.
Work from ** to ** again.

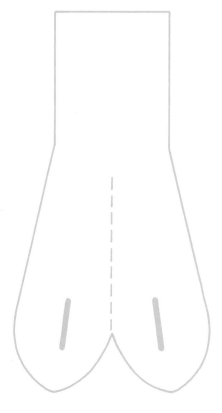

Press braces. Cut 8 shapes in felt or leather from the template plus one diamond shape with 3.5cm sides.
Machine sew 2 pieces together 3mm from the edge.
Rep for the other 6 shapes to make 4 tabs altogether. On wrong side mark buttonholes. Machine around mark and cut. Machine each end of knitted strip to a tab. Cross strips 20cm from ends and stitch on diamond shape.

Belt
With A, cast on 10 sts. Work as given for braces for 80cm.
Cast off in A.

Machine elastic to wrong side of belt along both edges.
Thread ends through buckles and firmly sew down 6cm overlap at each end.
Press with a warm iron.

Chequers pattern

1st row (RS) *K3B, K3A, rep from * to end.
2nd row *P3A, K3A, rep from * to end.
3rd row *P3A, K3A, rep from * to end.
4th row *P3B, K3A, rep from * to end.
5th row *K3A, P3B, rep from * to end.
6th row *K3B, P3A, rep from * to end.

These 6 rows form the pattern repeat.

Striped bar pattern

1st and 2nd rows With B, P.
3rd row (RS) With A, K.
4th row With A, P.
5th and 6th rows As 1st and 2nd rows using C instead of B.
7th and 8th rows As 3rd and 4th rows.
9th and 10th rows As 1st and 2nd rows using D instead of B.
11th and 12th rows As 3rd and 4th rows.
13th and 14th rows As 1st and 2nd rows using E instead of B.
15th and 16th rows As 3rd and 4th rows.
These 16 rows form the full pattern repeat.

Chapter 3
C·O·L·L·A·R·S, T·I·E·S
& S·C·A·R·V·E·S

Changing the neckline is an easy way of transforming an outfit. Add beads, lace or embroidery to a plain collar and turn it into a pretty frame for your face; put a frivolous bow tie with a shirt to give it a carnival air; add a beaded fichu or an embroidered scarf to a simple sweater or blouse and it becomes glamorous evening wear, or warm up your outdoor clothes with a colourful Fair Isle scarf or a crafty fun fox.

Collars and trims constantly change with the fashions, so keep an eye on the trends and regularly check through your wardrobe, revamping old outfits by adding new trims.

Pearl collar

Wear this exquisite beaded collar with a simple round-necked dress or a fine lambswool jumper for a really elegant look.

You will need: 20cm of 90cm-wide white lawn, 1200-1400 white pearls (depending on size), a press stud and one reel of white cotton thread.

Scale up the collar pattern piece. Place it right side up on white lawn and cut two pieces. Place it face down on fabric and cut two pieces.

Place two pieces right sides together and machine stitch 7mm from the raw edges, leaving the top edge open. Repeat for the remaining two pieces.

Clip the curves and turn collar pieces through to the right side, easing the seam on to the edge of the collar.

Cut 3cm-wide bias strips from remaining fabric and join to make a 50cm length. Fold 3mm to the wrong side along each long edge and press. Fold strip in half lengthwise, wrong sides together and press.

Arrange collar pieces side by side, with two fronts meeting at the centre. Tack loosely together.

With the right side of the binding to the underside of the collar, raw edges level and binding extending past the ends of the collar, tack binding to collar pieces along the crease line. Machine stitch.

Turn binding to the right side of collar so the folded edge just covers previous stitching line, tack and topstitch along the edge.

Sew the pearls to the collar one by one, using back stitch. Start at the back of one collar piece and work along the edge of the binding and around the curved edge. Continue working towards the centre, keeping beads close together. Repeat on the second collar piece.

Trim binding to extend 1.5cm from each side of collar at centre back. Turn in 5mm and slipstitch ends securely to neaten. Sew one half of press stud to each side.

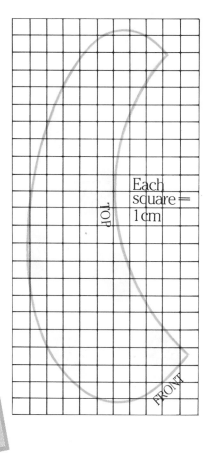

Each square = 1cm

TOP

FRONT

Hanky collars

A hanky collar with a decorative motif or an especially pretty border pattern makes an ideal collar for a little girl's dress.

You will need: a pocket hanky with a motif or attractive border; a round-necked dress; matching or contrasting bias binding, and matching thread.

Make up a round-necked dress of your choice according to the pattern instructions, leaving the neck edge unfinished. Alternatively, take a dress you already have and carefully remove the old collar or neck binding to expose the raw neck edges.

Fold the hanky in half across the width, horizontally and diagonally to see which looks more attractive. A horizontal fold will give a rectangular collar and a diagonal fold a diamond-shaped one.

Once you have decided on the shape of the collar, press the hanky lightly along the fold to mark the shoulder line. Fold it in half in the opposite direction and press again to mark centre front and centre back lines.

Make a cut along the centre back line, from the edge of the hanky to the centre (A-B).

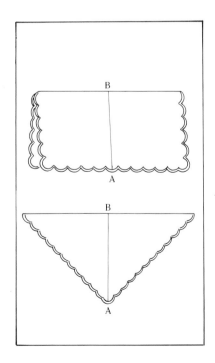

Put the dress on a coat hanger and arrange it so that it hangs properly. Place the collar over the dress so that the shoulder-line crease on the hanky aligns with the shoulder seams on the dress. The shape of the neck will show clearly through the fine lawn fabric of the hanky.

Pin the hanky to the dress, placing the pins just outside the neckline, and at right angles to it. Tack around the neckline and cut away the centre of the hanky, starting at the centre back opening and following the edge of the neck. Snip into the curved seam.

Neaten the raw edges at the centre back opening of the collar with a tiny rolled hem. Pin bias binding around the neck, with right sides together, and stitch in the crease line. Finger press the seam flat, and then turn completely to wrong side for an invisible finish, or use as a binding to complement the hanky design. Slipstitch in place at the wrong side of the neck, tucking in the raw ends. Alternatively, you could extend the binding at either side into ties, for a pretty bow. On a plainer hanky you could stitch a row of small buttons down the front, or on a party frock, sew tiny beads or pearls around the neck.

Poncho collar
cut 1 suede
cut 1 interfacing

1 square = 2.5 cm

Poncho

Appliqué a simple circular collar on to a mohair poncho, picking out the colours in the design to complement that of the fabric. A simple device, but effective.

You will need: 1.5m of 1.50cm-wide mohair fabric, 7m of matching 2.5cm-wide braid and matching thread, 40cm x 50cm each of suede and firm iron-on interfacing, scraps of leather, tapestry wool in four colours, a leather needle, fabric adhesive, pinking shears, and a leather hole punch.

Draw up the pattern from the graph and cut out the collar. Also make a pattern for the neck opening.

Work two lines of tacking stitches to divide fabric into quarters. Fold the fabric along tacking stitch lines, pin to

hold and trim corners to a curve. Bind the edges with braid. Matching neck opening pattern to intersection of tacking lines, cut out neck opening. Cut centre front slit to a depth of 12cm. Bind edges of neck opening and centre front slit with braid.

Iron interfacing to wrong side of suede collar. Punch holes 1.5cm apart around all the edges. Using trace pattern and pinking shears, cut out 13 leather triangles. Glue to the collar as shown.

Using leather needle and tapestry wool in three colours, work three fly stitches above triangles. Using fourth colour, join collar to poncho, with cross stitch worked through the punched holes and over the neck edge. Then work zigzag stitch in the same way around outside edge of collar.

Fly stitch

Bring the needle out at the left of the stitch, hold it down with the left thumb, and reinsert it a little to the right on the same level. Take a small diagonal stitch back into the centre and bring the needle out over the working thread. Pull the thread through and make a small stitch at the base of the V-shape to secure the loop.

Collar trims

Various fabrics and trimmings can be combined to transform dresses and blouses. Add a plain or embroidered collar to a patterned dress, or a patterned collar to a plain one, and update your old dresses by revamping the collars.

This pretty cotton print (left) is trimmed with a pre-gathered edging to complement the fabric. A plain white collar (below) is decorated with a simple embroidery design of bullion knots, worked in two strands of stranded cotton.

The pink polka-dot cotton collar bottom left is finished with a narrow broderie Anglaise edging. A small check gives a totally different look. The checked seersucker (bottom) is edged with ric-rac braid arranged to form a neat scalloped edge.

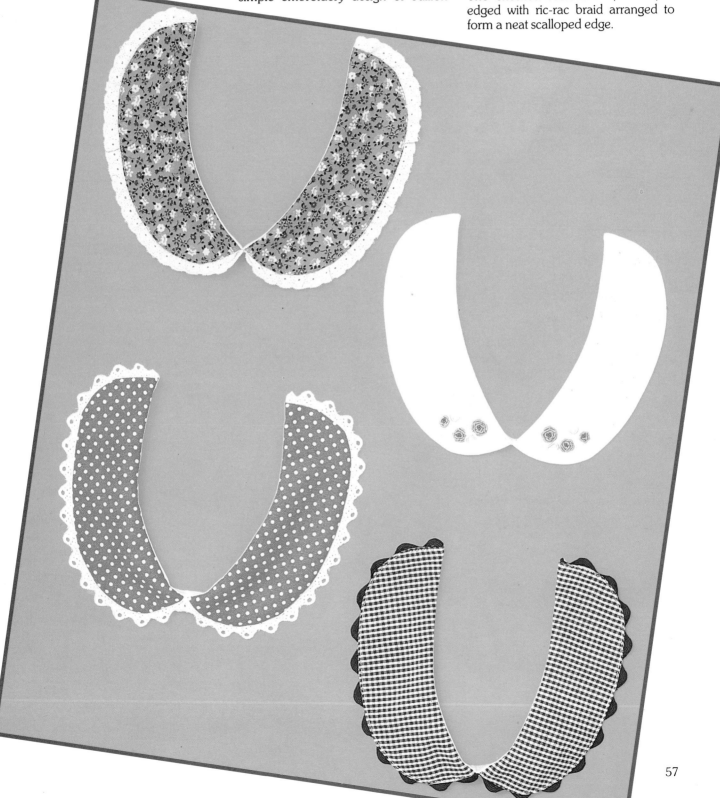

Ties and bows

Turn the conventional image upside down and use ties and bows in bright colours and snappy designs to give your shirts a frivolous air.

For the evenweave bow tie (1) you will need: 20cm of 90cm-wide evenweave linen and matching thread; 10cm of 90cm-wide light-weight interfacing; 20cm of 19mm-wide elastic; embroidery threads in the colours of your choice and two hooks and eyes.

Embroider the linen with straight stitches and curved trailing stitches (lay a thread across the linen in a curve and cover it with satin stitching).

Draw up the pattern from the graph in which one square equals 3cm and cut from fabric and interfacing.

Place each pair of fabric pieces with right sides facing with one piece of interfacing on the top of each pair. Taking a 5mm seam and leaving a gap for turning, pin, tack and stitch each fabric sandwich all around. Clip the seams, turn the fabrics right side out and press. Slipstitch the openings.

Turn in the narrow end of one half of the bow-tie, and stitch hooks to the wrong side. Insert elastic into the other end and stitch securely into place. Tie the bow-tie. Cut the elastic to the required length to fit neck. Turn in the second end of the elastic and sew on eyes to match the hooks.

Variations
Fabric bow-tie
Using the pattern for the eavenweave tie, make a fabric bow-tie from a bright, colourful print to match your skirt or trousers, or to co-ordinate with other accessories **(2)**.

Net bow-tie
Make a bow-tie from two 5cm x 12cm rectangles of pink net and trim it with beads, as shown, scattering them over the surface and outlining the edge **(3)**. Slipstitch the bow to an elastic band.

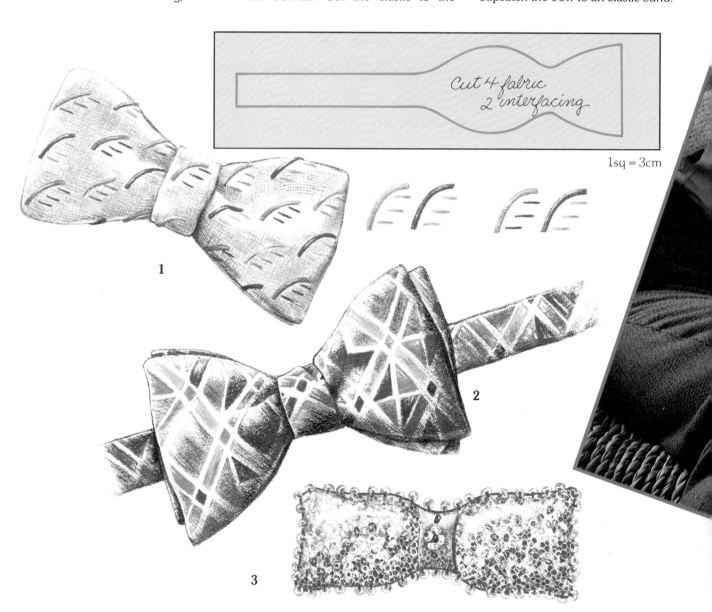

Cut 4 fabric
2 interfacing

1sq = 3cm

1

2

3

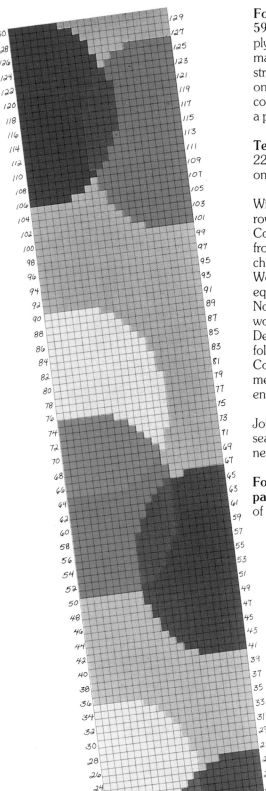

For the spotted tie (shown on page 59) you will need: two 50g balls of 3 ply wool, cotton or wool/silk mixture in main colour (A); two skeins of Anchor stranded cotton in contrast colour (B); one skein in each of five contrast colours (C), (D), (E), (F) and (G), and a pair of 3mm knitting needles.

Tension
22 sts and 34 rows to 10cm over st st on 3mm needles

With A, cast on 23 sts and beg with a K row work 10 rows st st.
Cont in st st working in colour patt from chart, twisting yarns tog when changing colour to avoid a hole.
Work 130 rows from chart (the square equals one stitch).
Now cont in A only, beg with a K row work 50 rows st st.
Dec 1 st at each end of next and every foll 10th row until 17 sts rem.
Cont without shaping until work measures 145cm from cast-on edge, ending with a P row. Cast off.

Join long seam and fold tie so that seam is at centre back. Join short ends neatly.

For the Argyll pattern tie (shown on page 59) you will need: one 20g ball of 3 ply wool, cotton or wool/silk

mixture in main colour (A), one ball each in contrast colours (B) and (C), a small amount of 4 ply gold glitter yarn and a pair of 3mm needles.

Tension
28 sts and 36 rows to 10cm over st st on 3mm needles

Divide the balls of A, B and C in half to give 6 small balls.
With A, cast on 29 sts. Beg with a K row cont in st st working in colour patt from chart (the square equals one stitch), using a separate ball for each colour section and twisting yarns tog to avoid a hole.
Cont until 200 rows have been worked from chart.
Keeping patt correct dec 1 st at each end of next and every foll 10th row until 23 sts rem.
Cont without shaping until 234 rows have been worked from chart.
Now cont in st st in stripe sequence of 10 rows A, 10 rows B, 10 rows C until work measures 145cm from cast-on edge, ending with a P row.
Cast off.

To make up
Following chart Swiss darn diagonal lines with the glitter yarn. Join long seam and fold tie so that seam is at centre back. Join short ends.

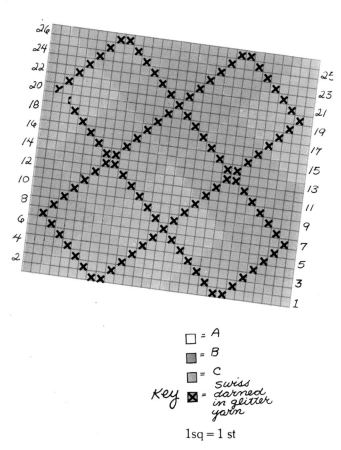

Key
A
B
C
D
E
F
G

1sq = 1 st

Key ☒ = swiss darned in glitter yarn
☐ = A
☐ = B
☐ = C

1sq = 1 st

Painted ties

For a really individual look, paint your own tie. Copy the design for a cheerful holiday tie shown here, or the skyscraper tie shown overleaf, or create your own unique picture tie.

For the holiday tie or the skyscraper tie you will need: 80cm each of 90cm-wide silk and lining fabric, matching thread, dressmaker's carbon paper, Dylon fabric paints in assorted colours, paintbrushes and (for the skyscraper tie only – see overleaf) a toothbrush.

Holiday tie

Draw up the pattern from the diagram overleaf and cut one each in silk and lining fabric.

Draw up the design from the coloured graph overleaf and transfer the outlines to the tie front. Using fabric paints and a fine brush, fill in the colours on

1sq = 3cm

68 cm.

16.5 cm.

Place on straight grain

14.5 cm.

Many up to similar notches on other side

1.5 cm.

13 cm.

55 cm.

1 cm

21 cm.

65 cm.

14 cm.

15.5 cm.

28 cm.

Place on straight grain

14.5 cm.

75.5 cm.

the tie front. Allow the paints to dry thoroughly and press well.

With right sides facing and taking a 1cm seam, join the two halves of the tie along the centre seam line. Repeat for the lining. Folding along the dotted lines turn in the ends of the tie and the

lining. Fold along dotted lines down the tie and taking 2cm seam join the back seam. Repeat for the lining taking a slightly larger seam.

Turn pieces right side out and press. Slip the tie over the lining and catch-stitch at either end.

Leather tie

Make this leather tie for your man or wear it yourself, contrasting it with a soft silk shirt. You could even use oddments to make matching leather earrings.

You will need: a 20cm x 80cm piece of leather for the basic tie and scraps in contrasting colours for the decorative motifs; matching threads; iron-on bonding; tracing paper, and a pencil.

Draw up the pattern pieces from the graph, in which one square equals 2.5cm, and cut out as indicated.

Trace off the outlines for the decorative shapes and cut them from the scraps of leather in contrast colours.

Position the motifs as shown and using a small, medium-spaced zigzag stitch and matching thread, stitch in place.

With right sides facing and taking a 5mm seam, join the two halves of the tie on the bias, as indicated.

Using a warm iron and pressing over two layers of paper, press the seam open. Fold in the sides of the tie along the lines indicated and, working in the same way, press the sides into place with iron-on bonding.

Skyscraper tie

Draw up the tie pattern and cut out the pieces, then transfer the design outlines to the tie front, as for the holiday tie.

Dip the toothbrush in red dye and flick it over the bottom half of the skyscraper area.

Working in the same way, flick blue dye over the top half of the skyscrapers, fading out approximately 20cm above the plane. Using the paintbrush, fill in the windows of the buildings and the plane and highlight with flashes of white fabric paint. Fill in the background areas of the buildings with dark fabric paints, as shown. Working with a toothbrush, as before, flick white paint over the buildings for highlights. Allow paint to dry then press with a hot iron to fix the fabric paints.

Make up the tie, following the instructions for the holiday tie.

1sq = 2cm

1sq = 2.5cm

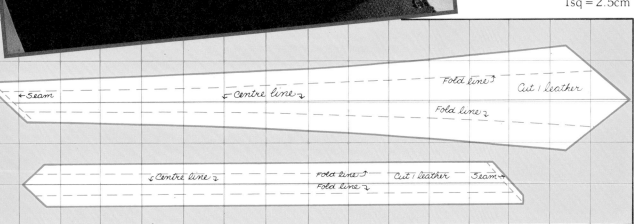

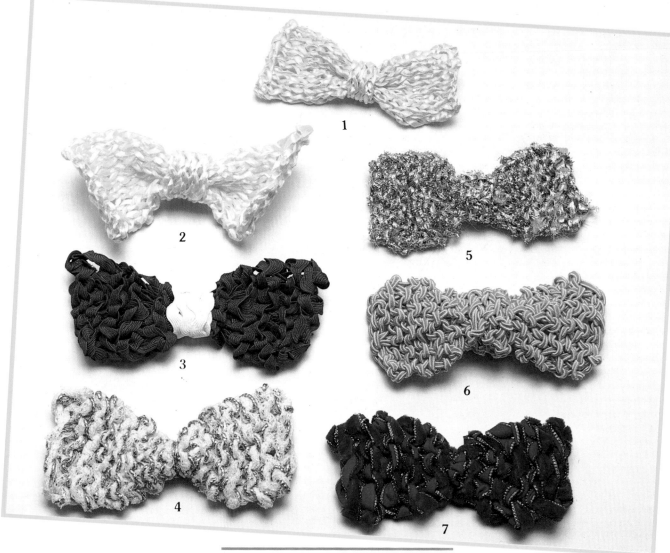

Novelty bows

Knit yourself a range of bows in ribbons, cords and braids and use them to trim the necklines of blouses, shirts and plain wool dresses.

All these bows are worked from ribbons, lace, ric-rac and other materials. Fastenings can be secured at the back of the work and can be worn as ties. If the ribbons are bought in short lengths, darn the ends in together at the back of the work once the bow is finished. Use a suitable pair of needles for each bow and work a small tension square before the main project. Change the needle size if the work does not look correct. Do not work the cast-on and cast-off edges tightly.

1 Ribbon bow
This is made from a polyester ribbon. Cast on the required number of stitches and work a rectangle in stocking stitch until bow measures the required length, and then cast off the stitches. In exactly the same way work a smaller rectangle for the centre. Stitch the smaller rectangle round the bow and stitch together at the back firmly.

2 Raffia bow
Use brightly coloured raffia to make this bow. The knitting must be worked at a loose tension, otherwise the work will curl. Work in the same way as the ribbon bow.

3 Ric-rac bow
Knit a length of ric-rac in garter stich to make this unusual bow. Use large needles and work a loose tension. Darn ends together neatly at back of work. Using contrast ric-rac, wind around centre.

4 Lace and braid bow
Strips of polyester thin lace and gold braid are worked together for this pretty bow. To give a dense fabric work in garter stitch. Once the rectangle is worked, wind gold braid tightly around the centre.

5 Gold fabric bow
Cut a piece of gold fabric into narrow strips and shred each edge. Work a rectangle in garter stitch. Work a smaller rectangle for the centre and stitch neatly at the back of the work.

6 Gold cord
This is worked in a fairly thick cord. Best results can be produced by using large needles and garter stitch. Work this as for the polyester ribbon bow.

7 Velvet bow
Strong velvet ribbon is used for the bow. Work a tight tension in garter stitch. Once a rectangle is worked, tie the centre with a cotton thread.

Evening bows

These elegant bow ties can be made in a couple of hours and are sure to give a party outfit a special touch.

You will need: 20cm of 90cm-wide fabric, matching sewing thread, silver thread for the embroidered tie and 80cm of elastic.

Cut piece of fabric 14cm x 12.5cm and fold it in half widthways, right sides together. Machine stitch 5mm from the edge, leaving a 5cm opening. Trim corners and turn right side out. Slipstitch opening to close. Press. Cut piece of fabric 11.5cm x 10cm. Fold and stitch as before. Press.

Mark small circles on right side of small rectangle and fill with satin stitch in silver. Gather centre of each bow with a small running stitch, fasten off. Place the wrong side of the smaller bow on the right side of the larger one and stitch together by hand at centre.

Cut a piece of fabric 5cm x 3cm. Fold it in half lengthways. With right sides together, and stitch 5mm from long edge, leaving ends open. Turn right side out and neaten one end. Press seam to centre back.

Cut a piece of elastic, 1cm longer than comfortably fits your neck outside a collar. Overlap ends by 1cm at centre back of bow tie and stitch in place. Wrap the loop round the centre of the tie and cut to length, allowing 1cm overlap. Lap the neatened end over the raw edge and stitch neatly together, catching them to the back of the tie.

Pearly bow tie

This ultra-feminine version of the bow tie would be perfect with a black evening dress.

You will need: 179 of 5mm round pearl beads, a pearl drop, 3m fuse or beading wire and a brooch clip.

Following the diagram, thread two beads on to the wire and slide to the centre. Thread the beads for the second row on to one end of the wire and push the other end of wire through the beads in the opposite direction. Pull both ends of the wire tight and adjust the beads so that they lie flat and straight. Continue in this way, working from A to C.

When the threading is complete, fold the bow tie along the lines indicated. Twist the wire to hold the front and back together at B. Thread one end of the wire through a 2cm pearl drop, through a 5mm round pearl and back up through the drop.

Pull the two ends of wire tightly and use to fasten a brooch clip to the back of the bow tie. Trim and tuck the ends of wire into the beadwork.

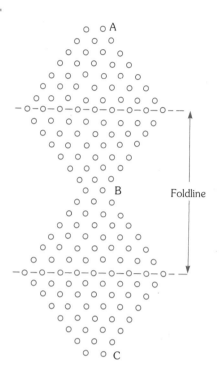

Beaded fichu

Transform a plain black sweater into evening wear with this glamorous gold and black fichu.

You will need: a 20g ball of Pingouin Place Vendôme, 450 x 8mm beads, a pair of 3¼mm knitting needles and a press stud.

Tension
21 sts and 46 rows to 10cm over g st

Thread all the beads on to yarn.
Cast on 1 st.
1st row Move bead up close to work (M bd), yon, K1 to sec bead.
2nd row M bd, yon, K1 to sec, K to end. Rep the 2nd row until there are 16 sts.
Next row M bd, yon, K1 to sec, K6, M bd and K1, called bd 1 K8. Rep the 2nd row 3 times.
Next row M bd, yon, K1 to sec, K5, bd 1, K to last 8 sts, bd 1, K to end. Rep 2nd row 3 times. Rep last 4 rows twice more.
Next row M bd, yon, K1 to sec, K5, bd 1, K8, bd 1, K8, bd 1, K7. Rep 2nd row 3 times.

Next row M bd, yon, K1 to sec, K5, bd 1, K7, bd 1, K to last 16 sts, bd 1, K7, bd 1, K7. Rep 2nd row 3 times. Rep last 4 rows twice more.
Next row M bd, yon, K1 to sec, K5, bd 1, K7, bd 1, K8, bd 1, K7, bd 1, K7. Rep 2nd row 3 times.
Next row M bd, yon, K1 to sec, K5, (bd 1), K7 twice, bd 1, K to last 24 sts, bd 1, K7) 3 times. Rep 2nd row 3 times. Rep last 4 rows twice. Cont in

this way, introducing a new 'V' of beads on next and every foll 16th row, maintaining lines of beads at 7 st intervals as set and inc 1st at beg of every row to 138 sts.
Next row M bd, yon, K1 to sec, (K4, bd 1) to last 2 sts, K2. Cast off.
Sew press stud to top corners.

Embroidered scarf

Embroider a plain woollen scarf to make the perfect accessory for a summer's evening, copying the design shown here or creating your own pattern to match your outfit.

1 sq = 2cm

French knots

Whipped running stitch

Detached chain stitch

Couching

Long and short stitch

Split stitch

French knots

Couching

Whipped running stitch

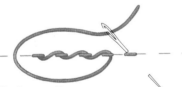

Work small even running stitches along the stitch line. Then bring the needle out just below the last stitch and work a return journey slipping the needle under the next stitch, taking care not to pierce the fabric. Use a tapestry needle for the whipping stitch and a contrasting coloured thread.

Split stitch

This is worked in a similar way to the more familiar stem stitch, except that the needle splits the thread of the previous stitch as it is brought out of the fabric, producing an effect rather like chain stitch.

Detached chain stitch

Work as ordinary chain stitch, holding the thread down to form a loop before reinserting needle at starting point. Bring needle through and make a small stitch over end of loop to finish.

French knots

Bring thread out and hold down to left. Twist thread twice round needle, insert it into fabric close to starting point. Pull through to back, tightening knot.

Long and short stitch

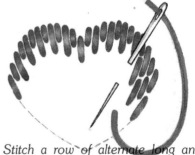

Stitch a row of alternate long and short satin stitches keeping outer edge even. Fill in shape working equal length stitches.

Simple couching

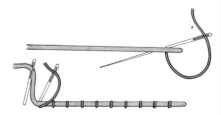

Bring out thread to be couched and lay it along stitch line. With a finer thread, work small stitches over laid thread.

Cat scarves

Children will love to choose between the elegant white cat or the ginger tom to wear for fun on autumn days.

For the white cat you will need: four 25g balls of Argyll Finesse mohair in Iceberg; oddments of black, pink and silver yarns; a pair of 5½mm knitting needles; a pair of false eyelashes; a length of narrow pink ribbon, and a piece of grey felt for paws.

For the ginger tom you will need: three 25g balls each of Argyll Finesse in Emberglow (A) and Tuscan (B); oddments of black, silver and white yarns, a pair of 5½mm knitting needles; a length of narrow orange ribbon, and a piece of black felt for boots.

Tension
16 sts and 22 rows to 10cm over st st on 5½ mm needles

White cat

Beg at tail. Using 5½mm needles, cast on 9 sts.
Starting with a K row, work in st st for 34cm, ending with a P row.
Cast on 8 sts at beg of next 4 rows. (41 sts.) ** Work 2cm in st st. Mark both ends of last row with a coloured marker. Work 5cm in st st. Mark both ends of last row with a coloured marker. ** Rep from ** to ** once more.
Work a further 28cm straight in st st from the coloured marker. Rep from ** to ** twice. Now work straight in st st for 12cm. Cast off.

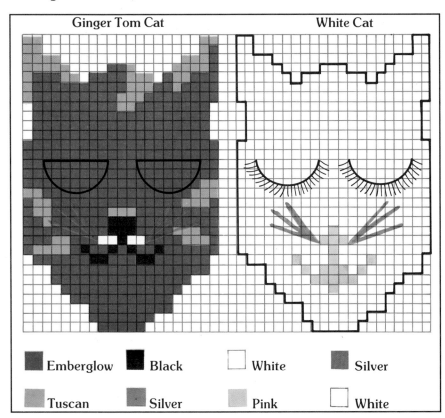

Ginger Tom Cat	White Cat

■ Emberglow	■ Black	☐ White	■ Silver
■ Tuscan	■ Silver	■ Pink	☐ White

For the legs: with right side of work facing and using 5½mm needles, pick up and K8 sts between the first two marked rows along the side edge. Beg with a P row, work 7cm in st st.
Dec 1 st at beg of next 4 rows. Cast off rem sts.
Work rem 7 leg pieces between rem 7 sts of markers.

For the face: using 5½mm needles cast on 3 sts. Starting with a K row, work in st st, at the same time inc 1 st at each end of the next 2 rows.
Cast on 2 sts at beg of foll 2 rows.
Rep the last 4 rows once more then inc 1 st at each end of next row. (21 sts.)
Work 11 rows straight in st st.
Now dec 1 st at each end of the next row.
Work 3 rows straight.
Inc 1 st at each end of foll row.
Work 1 row straight.

Divide for ears
Next row: K6, turn, cont on these sts only. ***
Dec 1 st at beg of next row (inner edge) and at the same edge on foll row. Cast off 2 sts at beg of next row.

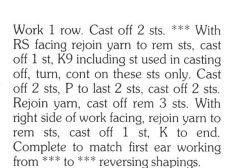

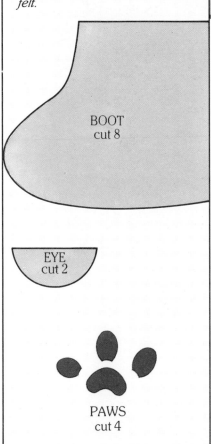

Trace off patterns for boots, eyes and paws. Cut out tips to fit ears in felt.

BOOT
cut 8

EYE
cut 2

PAWS
cut 4

Work 1 row. Cast off 2 sts. *** With RS facing rejoin yarn to rem sts, cast off 1 st, K9 including st used in casting off, turn, cont on these sts only. Cast off 2 sts, P to last 2 sts, cast off 2 sts. Rejoin yarn, cast off rem 3 sts. With right side of work facing, rejoin yarn to rem sts, cast off 1 st, K to end. Complete to match first ear working from *** to *** reversing shapings.

For the back head: work as given for face.
Join tail body and legs. Embroider the face details from the correct chart. Use the Swiss darning technique and embroidery stitches to make up the face. Using a strong clear adhesive stick on the false eyelashes. With the right side of the work facing, join the edges of the face to back of the head, leaving a small opening. Form open neck end of body into a circle and stitch to the back of the head. Tie the ribbon into a bow and stitch it neatly in front of one ear. Cut out felt shapes and stitch on for paws.

Ginger Tom
Work as given for white cat, but at the same time work body and legs in stripes throughout of 4 rows A, 4 rows B.
Work the face in A. The back head is worked in B.

Make up as given for white cat, embroidering the face details from the chart. Stitch a ribbon around the neck. Using black felt cut around the boot pattern. Stitch the pairs of boot sections together using a neat back stitch. Embroider large running stitches for the laces using a gold thread.
Cut out two semi-circles for the eyes and stitch neatly in position.

Fair Isle scarf

Winter coats tend to match the colours of leaden winter skies, so cheer up cold days with a stylish but warm and colourful Fair Isle scarf – the perfect gift for your family and friends.

You will need: five 50g balls of Pingouin Confortable in main colour (A) and one ball each in contrast colours (B), (C), (D), (E), (F), (G) and (H); one 20g ball of Pingouin Place Vendôme in contrast colour (J); a pair of 3½mm knitting needles, and a crochet hook.

Tension
21sts and 27 rows to 10cm over st st on 3½mm needles.

Using 3½mm needles and A, cast on 94 sts.
Beg with a K row work 2 rows in st st.
Commence patt panel, reading K rows from right to left and P rows from left to right.
1st row K61A, work 1st row from chart, K14A.
2nd row P14A, work 2nd row from chart, P61A.
These 2 rows establish the patt.

Keeping patt panel correct, cont until 330 rows have been worked from the beg.
Cont in A only.
Work 2 rows st st. Cast off.

Join side seam and ends of scarf.
Make tassels and loop through ends of scarf with crochet hook.

A D G

B E H

C F J

Fun fox

This cunning fun fox stole made in silver fur fabric is as kind on your pocket as it is to animals. Wear it with smart, simple clothes for the maximum effect.

You will need: 1.40m x 65cm of silver polished short pile fur fabric, 20cm x 20cm of black short pile fur fabric, 40cm of 115cm-wide silver satin lining fabric, 1.10m of 90cm-wide cotton domette, a wad of cotton wool the size of your hand; two 12mm blue safety eyes, one 15mm black animal nose, one mink clip or clothes peg and a teasel brush.

Note: If you are not used to sewing fur fabrics, practise on scraps before making the fox. Use between 8 and 10 stitches to 2.5cm and, after stitching, clip away the surface pile from the seam allowances to reduce bulk. Try finger pressing the seams, but if this does not work, use a well padded ironing board and a cool iron, and experiment with an oddment before pressing the seam.

Scale up the pattern from the grid, using dressmaker's graph paper (1cm seam allowances are included in the pattern).

Lay the pattern pieces on the wrong side of the fur fabric as shown in the cutting layouts, making sure that the pile of the fabric runs from nose to tail on all body and leg pieces, and upwards on the ear pieces. Cut two of the four ear pieces and two tail tips in

black. Pin pieces in place and cut out. Pin and cut out one underside body piece in lining fabric and one in cotton domette. Transfer all markings to fabric with tailor's tacks, including the positions of the eyes and ears on main body piece.

Make small holes in the fur fabric at the eye positions on the main body piece, using a knitting needle. Push the plastic eye pieces through the holes and fix from behind with the safety washers provided.

Reinforce V-shape at end of tail on main body and underside tail pieces with a row of staystitching on seamline. Clip to stitching at point. Pin, tack and stitch black tail tips to each tail

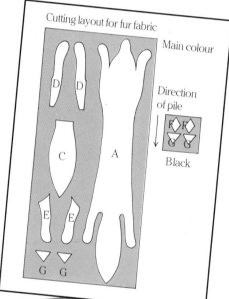

Cutting layout for fur fabric

Main colour

Direction of pile

Black

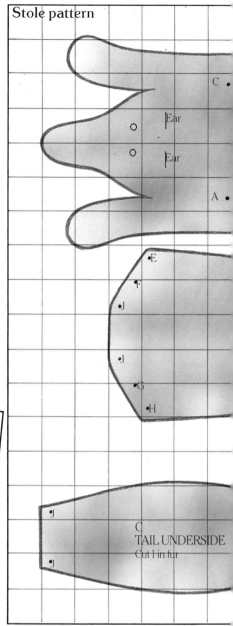

Stole pattern

piece, right sides together. Press.

With right sides together, attach front and back legs and tail to the underside of the body piece, matching equivalent markings. Pin and tack very carefully as the lining and fur fabric will tend to slide, then sew with a plain seam. Press the seam outwards, away from the body. Tack cotton domette to the wrong side of the underside body piece, matching markings.

With right sides together, pin and tack main body piece and underside together carefully along stitching line, leaving an opening between X markings for turning right side out. Trim seams close to the seamline and clip to points A, C, F and G to prevent puckering at the corners. Turn right side out through the opening, pushing

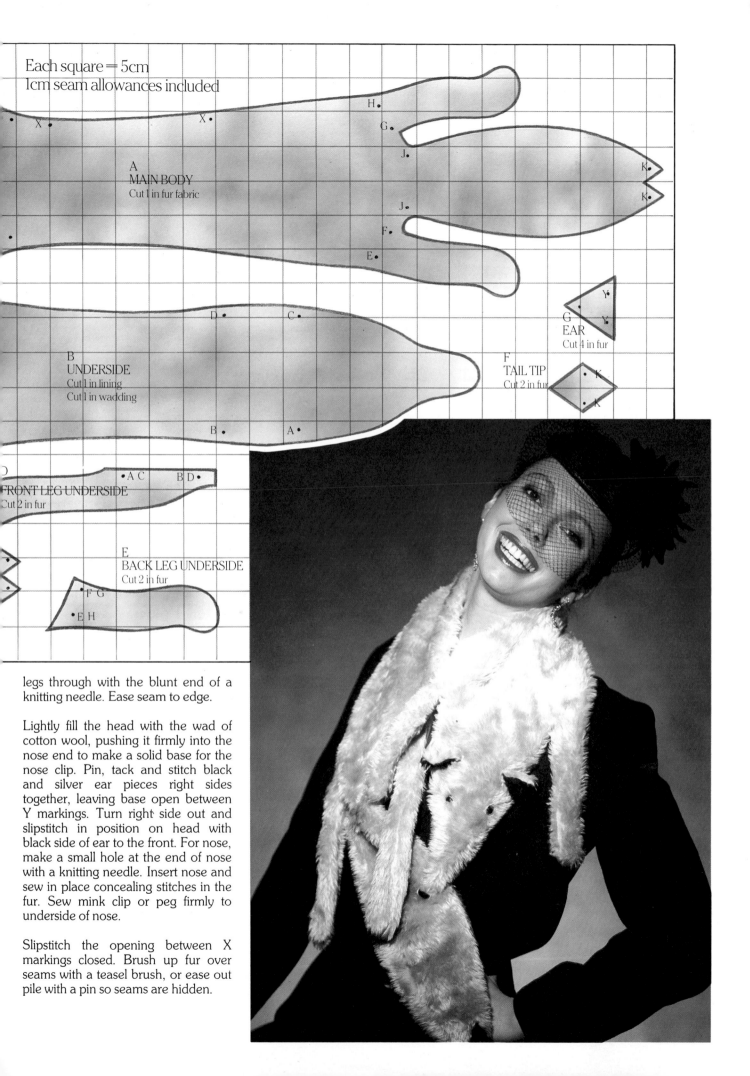

Each square = 5cm
1cm seam allowances included

X•   X•

H•
G•
J•
K•
K•

A
MAIN BODY
Cut 1 in fur fabric

J•
F•
E•

D•   C•

G•
Y•
G
EAR
Cut 4 in fur

B
UNDERSIDE
Cut 1 in lining
Cut 1 in wadding

F
TAIL TIP
Cut 2 in fur
•K
•K

B•   A•

D
•A C   B D•
FRONT LEG UNDERSIDE
Cut 2 in fur

E
BACK LEG UNDERSIDE
Cut 2 in fur

•F G
•E H

legs through with the blunt end of a
knitting needle. Ease seam to edge.

Lightly fill the head with the wad of
cotton wool, pushing it firmly into the
nose end to make a solid base for the
nose clip. Pin, tack and stitch black
and silver ear pieces right sides
together, leaving base open between
Y markings. Turn right side out and
slipstitch in position on head with
black side of ear to the front. For nose,
make a small hole at the end of nose
with a knitting needle. Insert nose and
sew in place concealing stitches in the
fur. Sew mink clip or peg firmly to
underside of nose.

Slipstitch the opening between X
markings closed. Brush up fur over
seams with a teasel brush, or ease out
pile with a pin so seams are hidden.

Chapter 4

H·A·T·S

Hats are the ultimate accessory, changing the shape of your face and transforming anything you wear into an outfit rather than a collection of clothes; making a bold statement about you, your image and your mood of the moment. Now that hats are back in fashion, make a good selection to suit your changing moods and clothes.

Making straw and felt hats is a specialist craft, but don't let this put you off: with a little imagination and some basic dressmaking skills you can create a host of soft hats ranging from snappy little berets to enchantingly frivolous cocktail hats, or simply buy the cheapest and simplest straw hat and turn it into your own creation by adding fabric flowers or by painting on it.

Butterfly beret

Take an ordinary beret and add a colourful appliqué motif, sequins and beads, for an original look.

You will need: a purchased beret, small scraps of Chinese silk or other fabric in three complementary colours, matching threads, a small amount of paper-backed bonding, 17 sequins and small beads to tone with the fabric colours.

Trace each of the outlines separately on to paper side of bonding and press on to the wrong side of the relevant fabrics. Cut out.

Remove the paper and arrange the shapes on the beret so that the lower tips of wings end about 1cm from the edge of the beret. Press to bond them in place.

Using a small, close zigzag stitch, stitch around the edge of the shapes, starting with the grey areas. Machine stitch the antennae with small zigzag stitch and finish ends securely on the wrong side.

Finish each antenna with a sequin and bead, stitching the bead through the centre of the sequin to hold it in place. Repeat at random over the surface of the beret for a sparkling effect .

Soft berets

It is easy to make your own beret rather than trimming a bought one, and the finished effect can vary from sporty and casual to elegantly formal.

For all three versions shown here and on page 78 you will need: 50cm of 90cm-wide lining fabric to match the main fabric, 50cm of 90cm-wide interfacing, 70cm of 4cm-wide petersham ribbon and matching thread.

For the tweed beret you will also need: 50cm of 71cm-wide Harris tweed and one feather (optional).

For the moiré beret you will also need: 50cm of 120cm-wide moiré taffeta and 1m of 23mm-wide satin ribbon.

Tweed beret

Measure the circumference of your head at its widest, just above the eyebrows. Make the pattern for the darted beret shown overleaf, drawing two circles with a 16cm radius for upper and lower brim sections, and folding the dart to take in 6.5cm at the outer stitching line. Cut out upper and lower brim sections and headband in tweed and stitch dart in upper brim section and seam in lower brim section. Make up as for basic beret, line and finish with a feather (optional).

Moiré beret

Determine your head size as above. Make the pattern for the basic beret described overleaf, drawing two circles with a 16cm radius for upper and lower brim sections. Cut both brim sections and headband in moiré. Cut and join 6cm wide bias strips to make a ring 1m in length. Join one edge to upper brim section and the other edge to lower brim section, taking 1.5cm seams. Make as for basic beret; line and trim with a flat ribbon bow.

77

Sailor hat

For the sailor hat you will also need:
50cm of 90cm-wide white cotton drill, 10cm of 90cm-wide navy cotton drill and red wool for a pompon.

Measure your head (see Tweed beret) and make the pattern for the basic beret as described overleaf, drawing one circle with a 13cm radius for the upper brim section and the second with a 12.5cm radius for the lower brim section. Cut the upper and lower brim sections in white cotton drill and the headband in navy cotton drill. Make up as described on the opposite page, line with lining fabric, and finish with a bright red pompon (see page 80).

Making a basic beret

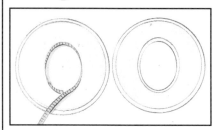

1 Cut two circles in stiff paper, the first with a radius of 13cm for the upper brim section and the second with a radius of 12.5cm for the lower brim section. Add 1.5cm seam allowance all round.

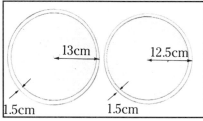

2 Draw an oval at the centre of the lower brim section to the size of your head plus 13mm ease, arranging a tape measure on its edge to give a good shape. Mark carefully, then draw a line 1.5cm inside the oval for the seam allowance. Cut out.

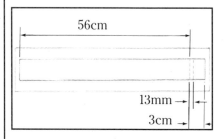

3 To make the headband pattern, mark out a strip 10cm wide, with the length equal to your head measurement, plus 13mm ease and 3cm for seam allowances. Cut out.

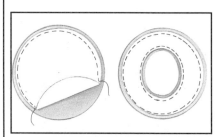

4 Cut upper and lower brim sections in fabric and interfacing and tack interfacing to wrong side of relevant pieces. Cut the headband in main or contrast fabric and petersham to length of headband pattern piece.

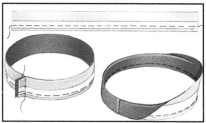

5 Fold fabric headband piece in half lengthwise with wrong sides together and press. Unfold, and tack petersham to wrong side with one edge level with crease line. Stitch ends together with right sides facing and press seam open. Fold headband in half again, with wrong sides together.

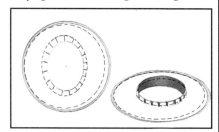

6 Staystitch lower brim section along stitching line of inner oval and clip to staystitching. Remove previous tacking. Pin raw edge of headband to clipped edge of lower brim section, with right sides together. Tack and stitch along the seamline.

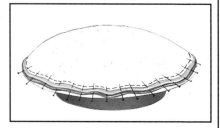

7 Gather outer edge of upper brim section using a large machine stitch. Place upper and lower brim sections right sides together and pin at right angles to raw edges. Pull up gathering thread slightly to ease. Tack and stitch along seamline.

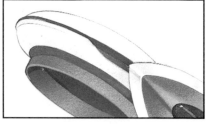

8 Trim seam and press open with the tip of the iron, holding the beret in the hand and pressing over a pad made of cloth or tissue paper. Turn the beret right side out and press again over a pad, as before.

Making a darted beret

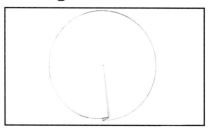

1 Cut two circles the required size in stiff paper and make an identical dart in each, by folding from the outer edge to the centre so the dart tapers to nothing at the centre point.

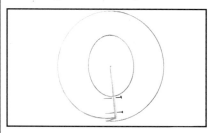

2 Take the pattern for the under brim section, fold the dart to one side and pin or stick in place with adhesive tape. Measure the oval shape at the centre of the under section as for the basic beret.

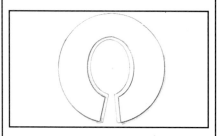

3 Open out the dart and cut along dart fold lines and oval to make a keyhole shape. Draw round this shape on another piece of paper and add 1.5cm seam allowance to dart edges and inner edge of oval.

4 To make up, cut out pieces in fabric and interfacing and tack interfacing to relevant pieces. Make dart in upper brim section, trim and press open. Stitch the seam in under the brim section and press open. Piece together as for the basic beret.

Pompon beret

Fourteen pompons in a mixture of two mohair yarns make a fluffy brim round the edge of this beret and act as a frame for the face, giving it height.

You will need: three 25g balls of mohair in main colour (A); two 25g balls of mohair in a contrast colour, a set of four 3½mm needles pointed at both ends for knitting in rounds, and cardboard for making the pompons.

Using A, cast on 12 sts, sl 4 sts on to 3 separate needles, work with the fourth needle.
Leave a length of yarn to draw up the hole afterwards.
1st round: K.
2nd round: K1B (pick up the bar below the next st on the left hand needle and K into the back of it) K1, K1B, K1, on each needle.
3rd round: K1B, K2, K1B, on each needle.
4th round: K1B, K3, K1B, on each needle.
5th round: K1B, K4, K1B, on each needle.
Inc in this way in every round until there are 32 sts on the needle.
Next round: K1B, K17, on each needle.
Next and every alt round: K.
Next round: K1B, K18, on each needle.
Next round: K1B, K19, on each needle.
Cont in this way until 29 rounds have been completed.
Next round: K1B, K22, K1B, on each needle.
Cont without further shaping for 10 rounds.
Cast off.

Using a darning needle and matching thread, gather the edge till it fits the head. To make the pompons, cut 2 pieces of card with a radius of 8cm and cut a smaller hole in the centre of both cards. Place the two pieces of card together. Using a mixture of both yarns, wind around the card till full. Cut through the centre of the two pieces and tie securely.
Make 14 pompons and sew around the edge of beret, at least 4cm from the cast-off edge.

Making pompons

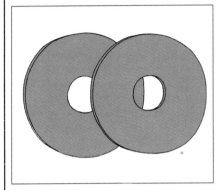

1 *Cut two circles of thin card the size required for the pompon. Cut out a smaller circle from centre of both pieces.*

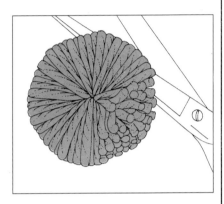

3 *Cut the yarn around outer edges of the circles, slipping the scissors between the two pieces of card.*

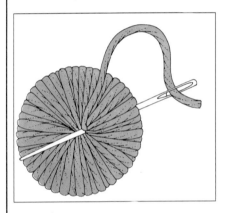

2 *Wind the yarn evenly around both pieces of card in the same direction until the hole is full. It may be easier to thread the yarn through the holes using a blunt-ended needle.*

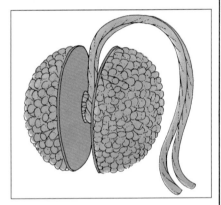

4 *Take a long length of yarn and tie securely around the centre of the pompon between the two pieces of card. Remove the card, and fluff out the pompon, trim if necessary.*

Cocktail hats

The ritzy little cocktail hat is fashionably to the fore once more. For the most enticing effect, wear one tilted elegantly well on to the forehead, either with the frill just above the eyes or with the veil dipped demurely below.

For the frilled teardrop you will need: 20cm x 20cm each of light brown panne velvet, spotted black net, black felt, milliner's buckram and polythene; 50cm of black pleated trim with a stiffened gold edge; one ball of goldfingering yarn; 10cm of 1.5cm-wide gold braid; matching sewing thread, and a wig stand or alternative round surface on which to shape the basic hat mould.

For the veiled teardrop you will need: 20cm x 20cm each of iridescent lurex, milliner's buckram, black felt, and black spotted hexagonal net; 50cm x 50cm of black spotted net; 50cm of black spotted pleated trim with a stiffened gold edge; gold fingering yarn; matching sewing thread, and a wig stand.

For the feathered teardrop you will need: 20cm x 20cm each of black spotted pink taffeta, black felt and milliner's buckram; 25cm of plain black pleated trim; gold fingering yarn; two royal blue marabou feathers, and matching sewing thread.

Note: If you cannot obtain any of the fabrics listed for a particular hat you can easily experiment with oddments of other fancy or unusual fabrics. For the basic shape, choose from iridescent lurex, taffeta, moiré, silk, satin, panne velvet, cotton pique or patterned lace. For the veil, experiment with different hexagonal nets which should be sufficiently soft to drape well over the face. Nets can be plain or spotted, in small or large repeats and with either small or large spots. The spots themselves may be woven flat or raised. Plain nets can be hand decorated with ribbon bows, beads, pearls tassels or braids.

Net does not fray, which means that the cut edges may be left unfinished. As an alternative to the veil, a ready-made trim makes an ideal edging. There are fine polyester net edgings, both plain and spotted, which can be bought already pleated or gathered with decorative wired edges. The stiffened edge can easily be manipulated to hold a particular shape well.

Frilled teardrop

First press the fabrics to remove all the creases. Trace off the basic teardrop shape given on page 84, completing the oval by reversing the shape on the centre line. Shape the buckram mould as shown. When it is completely dry, lift it off the curved surface and discard the polythene.

With the right side of the velvet uppermost, and the straight grain running the length of the oval, cover the curved side of the mould. Working from the underside, pin the fabric close to the edge, pinning first through the buckram. Trim the velvet around the edge and machine zigzag-stitch all round the basic teardrop.

Either hand couch, or use a narrow zigzag stitch to machine couch gold fingering into a spiral pattern. Begin in the middle with about 6mm between each spiral, increasing the spaces to about 1cm around the outer edge.

Next, cover the mould with the black net and stitch around the edge, as described for the velvet. Then, pin the felt lining in place and repeat, stitching around the edge as before.

To complete the hat, pin the pleated trim in place, about 1cm in from the edge. Overlap the two cut edges by 6mm and stitch together with a flat seam. Remember that when the trim is stitched to the hat it will curl in one direction, so make sure before stitching that it will curl upwards rather than downwards. Straight stitch around, first securing the edge of the trim, and then work a second row around the edge of the hat.

To make a bow, cut two pieces of felt each 5cm x 10cm and pink or scallop the short sides. Place the two pieces together, gather the middle and pin gold braid around. Machine stitch to

Moulding the basic shape

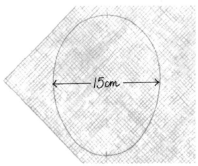

1 *Transfer the teardrop outline on to buckram across the grain of the fabric. Using sharp shears, cut out on the trace line.*

2 *Dip into warm water, sufficiently to dampen but not to saturate the buckram. With the fingers, ease out the fabric across the grain, releasing the stiffening agent.*

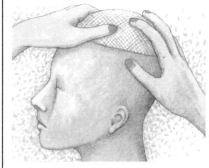

3 *Shape the buckram over a rounded surface such as a polystyrene wig stand. First, cover the stand with polythene and using both hands, press until the fabric holds a curved shape. Leave to dry naturally in a warm place.*

Basic teardrop pattern

centre line

hold and hand stitch bow to the back of the hat to finish. Secure hats in place with hat pins.

Veiled teardrop

Make the basic shape in exactly the same way as previously described, omitting the couched spiral pattern, then finish as follows.

Pin the hat in the centre of the net (on the bias if preferred). Using tailor's chalk or fine stainless pins, mark an oval outline closely following the hat shape, and extending it to the outside edge of the net, see opposite.

Cut it out, and using a fine matching coloured thread, stitch it to the edge of it the hat. Apply gold fingering to the edge either by hand or machine.

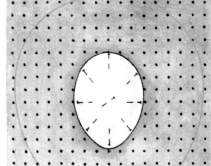

To make the rosettes, cut the pleated trim equally into three. Roll each length round quite firmly, pleating the fullness. Stitch to hold. Repeat for the second two rosettes, arrange them in a pleasing way, and machine stitch to the back of the hat, with the open ends facing towards the front.

Feathered teardrop

Make in exactly the same way as for the frilled teardrop as far as covering the mould with the main fabric.

Extend the lining by 1.5cm all round and turn the outside edge to the right side of the hat. Straight stitch in place, working the first row on the edge of the felt and the second row around the edge of the hat.

Apply gold fingering to cover the inner edge either by hand or machine. Shape the trim into a rosette as previously described and place the feathers in the fold. Stitch to hold and machine stitch to back of hat with open end of rosette and feathers facing the front of the hat.

Adapting the basic hat

This simple shape can be used to create an infinite number of hats for special occasions. Use wedding lace or bead-stitched slipper satin for a summer wedding or classic race meeting. Choose rich silk, taffeta, satin or layers of shiny net for a smart, chic effect, or leave off some of the more exotic trims for a neat little hat which would be perfect for a business lunch.

Some further suggestions are given on the following two pages using a mixture of fashion fabrics, from leather and net to lacy frills, – but it is more fun to try out your own ideas, experimenting with fabrics and trims which will complement your clothes.

White Russian

1 Interpret the latest frilly look with off-white silk and gilt-edged pleated trim. Lightly pad the basic hat shape and stitch with tiny glass beads.

Moulin bleu

2 Marabou feathers have always been favourite accessories. Arrange three on smoky grey panne velvet with a feather-trimmed brim.

Satellite

3 For a bolder, more trend-setting effect, use crisp silver net with several layers of blue and pink net and hold with twisted silk cord.

Pink fizz

4 For a cool, crisp effect, use fine pink and white striped cotton piqué and finish with a snappy bow stitched to one side of the hat.

Old Venice

5 For a light, summery look, use a layer of lace (either old or new) over a plain cotton background and trim with pleated lace edging.

Blue ice

6 For this individual effect, use blue moiré silk and net. Top the hat with a large flower edged with pink and stiffened tubular rayon for the stamen.

Party hairbands

These sparkling hairbands take hardly a moment to make and create an instant party atmosphere. Wear the striped band with the bow to the side, as here, or wear the plaited band for a softer more romantic effect.

For the striped hairband you will need: 60cm x 20cm of striped lamé, two pieces of light-weight iron-on interfacing measuring 2.5cm x 51cm and 2cm x 6cm, 20cm of 2cm-wide elastic and matching sewing thread.

For the plaited band you will need: approximately 30cm x 30cm each of black fabric and gold and pink lurex fabric, matching threads, a ball of goldfingering, double knitting wool, a darning needle, and a press stud.

Striped hairband

For the bow, cut a rectangle of fabric 15.5cm x 13cm, with stripes parallel with short edge. Turn 5mm to wrong side of each short edge and press. Fold fabric right sides together so the pressed edges meet at the centre and machine the raw edges together at each end with a 5mm seam. Turn through and press. Slipstitch opening to close.

For the band, cut two 6cm-wide bias strips from remaining fabric. With right sides together, join strips with a 5mm seam and press open. Trim the length of fabric to 51cm, keeping the seam in the centre.

Apply interfacing to the centre of the wrong side of the band. Press. Turn over 5mm to the wrong side of each long

edge and press. Fold to the centre as before and slipstitch the opening. Turn in raw edges at each end to neaten and slot in ends of elastic, adjusting to fit head. Stitch both ends through all layers.

Gather centre of bow from top to bottom and draw up to measure 2.5cm. Stitch bow to right side of band 2.5cm away from centre.

For the bow knot, cut a piece of fabric 6cm square. Press small strip of interfacing to the centre on the wrong side, following direction of stripes. Turn 5mm to the wrong side of the edges above and below interfacing and press. Fold to centre, overlapping edges, and slipstich opening. With

seam inwards, stitch one raw edge of strip to centre back. Turn in other edge 5mm, bring round front of bow and slipstitch to back over raw edge.

Plaited hairband

Cut 4cm-wide bias strips and join them to make 120cm length in each colour. Trim and press seams open. Fold each strip in half lengthwise and machine along centre. Turn right side out and thread with four strands of wool, using a darning needle. Secure the ends with a safety pin and plait the strips together.

Tie the plait to fit comfortably around the head by first wrapping one end around the other. Pin in position and remove from head. Attach a press stud to secure the tied plait in place as shown in the diagram opposite.

Unplait the ends and trim each one to between 10cm and 15cm from the knot, varying the lengths. Cut 3cm of wool from the ends of each rouleau and turn in raw edges.

Cut 3m length of goldfingering for each tassel and keep folding in half until it is 7cm in length. Bind the loop once or twice at the centre of its length with a doubled thread. Take the needle into the rouleau to pull the tassel 1cm or so in from the end of the tubing. Catch the ends of the rouleau together with very small stitches to secure tassel in place. Trim the tassels neatly.

Bridal headband & coronet

The enchanting bridal headband with its matching choker and the pretty bridesmaid's coronet look stunning but they are simple to make. Trim them with purchased flowers, as seen on the bridal coronet, or make your own, as described overleaf.

For the bridal headband and choker you will need: 20cm of 90cm-wide duchess satin, sewing thread, a hairband approximately 2cm wide, 40cm of 2cm-wide petersham, hooks and eyes and a selection of purchased silk flowers.

For the rosebud coronet you will need: 25cm of 22mm-wide single-faced polyester satin ribbon for each of the 11 larger rosebuds, 25cm of 16mm-wide ribbon for each of the 11 smaller rosebuds, wire stems, binding wire, green binding tape, artificial rose leaves and a lampshade ring 15cm in diameter, 50cm in circumference.

Note: If the bridesmaid's head is larger or smaller, the ring size and the number of flowers must be adjusted accordingly.

Headband and choker

Pin-tuck a section of fabric which measures approximately 50cm x 20cm across. This will be for the headband and choker. Make the pin tucks to measure approximately 3mm when finished with an even spacing of 2cm between each running diagonally across the strip of fabric.

For the headband, start by measuring the length and depth (underside and top side) of the hair band and draw a rectangle on a piece of paper to these measurements and add an extra 1cm to each side as a seam allowance.

Fine pin-tucking is used here to add an unusual texture to this matching bridal headband and choker. The pin-tucking is diagonal and silk flowers and ribbons add the final decoration.

Use this rectangle as your pattern piece and place on to fabric — with pin tucks running diagonally — and cut

out. Press 1cm seam allowances on each end of the rectangle towards the wrong side.

Cover the hair band with the pin-tucked rectangle — ensuring that the seam runs down the centre of the underneath side. Pin, tack and finish by hand sewing the fabric into place. To neaten the seam, sew a strip of remaining ribbon along the entire length of the seam.

Cut three lengths of ribbon each measuring approximately 50cm in length. Overlap the ends, attach to each side of the headband and hand sew neatly into place.

Arrange the flowers, covering ribbon ends, on the headband and sew securely.

For the choker, cut petersham to your neck circumference plus an overlap of approximately 1cm for fastening. Cut a pin-tucked section of fabric which measures the size of the choker with a 1cm seam allowance on all sides.

Place petersham on to the pin-tucked fabric and trim. Press back the 1cm seam allowance to the wrong side on both short ends of your rectangle and

one of the long sides. Cover the petersham with the seam running down the centre of the wrong side.

Place the pressed edge so that it overlaps the raw edge, pin and sew into place. Position the hooks and eyes for fastening and hand sew into place. Trim the overlapping edge of the choker with an arrangement of flowers.

For more elaborate decorative effects, stitch narrow pieces of lace along the edges of the pin tucks. Alternatively, emphasize tucks with small pearls or delicate beads stitched along the fold lines. Trim the flower and ribbon decorations of the headband and choker with lace and beads to match.

Rosebud coronet

Bind the lampshade ring tightly with binding tape. Take care that all parts of the ring are covered and none of the background colour shows through.

Work each rosebud as shown overleaf. Bind the lower edge of each ribbon rosebud with binding wire.

Cut an approximate 5cm length of wire for each rosebud stem and bend over the top 2cm of the wire. Neatly bind the bottom of each rosebud to the folded end of each stem.

Wind binding tape carefully around the base of each rosebud and the top half of the stem. Continue along the entire length of each wire stem.

Inserting leaves, as desired, bind the lower half of each rosebud stem to the circlet with binding wire. When all rosebuds are in place, bind the entire circlet with binding tape, covering and holding the remainder of each stem firmly in place. Make sure the rosebud stems are radiating from the centre. Gently bend the leaves into a realistic position, so that the wire undersides do not show. Angle the roses to face in different directions.

Making folded roses

Folded ribbon roses make delightful trims for hats and headbands. Experiment with spotted, striped and patterned ribbons as well as the more conventional plain colours.

For each rose you will need: 1m of gift or craft ribbon (the rosebuds on the preceding page only take 25cm because they are made to a smaller scale and the outside, opened-out petals are not included), binding wire, green binding tape and artificial rose leafs, if desired.

Note: Different widths of ribbon will produce different sized roses. A 3.5cm-wide ribbon will produce a 7cm rose; a 2cm ribbon a 5cm-wide rose.
If the roses are made from materials other than specialist fabrics, some difficulty may be found in binding the stems. The wires can be covered with fabric tape, bias binding or gift wrap ribbon, but these materials tend to slip during the winding process. To help overcome this, wrap strips of double-sided sticky tape round the wire first.

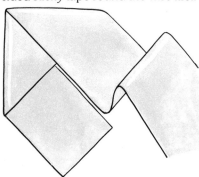

1 With the ribbon face up and leaving an end of approximately 5cm, fold over the ribbon to form a right angle. Fold the long end forward again to form another right angle.

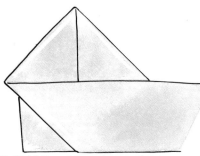

2 Fold the ribbon forward twice more at right angles to form a square shape.

3 Continue folding the ribbon at right angles to form square on top of square until all the ribbon is used up. Fold end of ribbon towards centre and trim away any excess as necessary.

4 Folding as necessary, thread the top end of the ribbon through a large-eyed needle. Holding the squares together tightly, push the needle down through the centre of the folded squares.

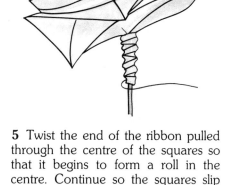

5 Twist the end of the ribbon pulled through the centre of the squares so that it begins to form a roll in the centre. Continue so the squares slip round against one another to form a perfect rose shape.

Fold over the end of the wire stem and bind the ends of the ribbon tight to it with binding wire. Bind the wire stem with tape, inserting a leaf close to the top, if desired.

Wired flowers

Wired flowers offer the opportunity to use a much wider range of fabrics than folded roses and the technique can be adapted to many different petal shapes.

For each flower you will need: suitable fabric (see note below); cotton-covered flowermaking wire; a tube between 1.5cm and 3.5cm in diameter (this will govern the size of the petals); clear drying adhesive; artificial stamens; thin binding wire; pliers; green gutta tape; artificial leaves (optional).

Note: Ribbons, dress-weight cottons and silks, broderie Anglaise, nets and lace: any fabric which does not easily fray is suitable for making flowers. Very delicate fabrics like lace or muslin can be starched first to give them a crispness or texture which will make them easier to use. Plain fabrics can be decorated with fabric paints.

1 Use pliers to bend the wire round the tube, and twist the ends together for three or four turns. Trim the short end of the wire, and cut off the excess wire, leaving it approximately 14cm long, or the required length.

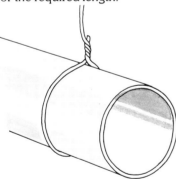

2 The circular wire shape can be kept for round petals, or gently pulled into an oblong, heart or triangle shape.

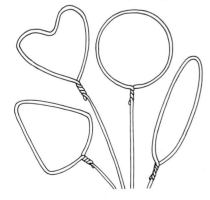

3 Bend the petal stem out of the way, and coat one side of wire shape sparingly with adhesive. Press the shape down on to the right side of the material, and leave to dry thoroughly for several hours, or overnight.

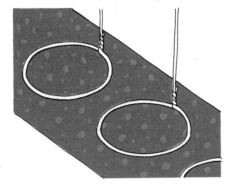

4 Cut away the excess fabric from the petal shape. Use sharp pointed scissors to cut as closely as possible to the wire petal shape.

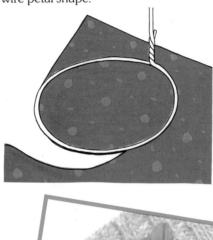

5 Take four stamens and bend them in half. Use binding wire to join them to the first petal. Add four other petals, one at a time, winding wire round each one individually. Finish by securing the five petals together and cut off the excess lengths of wire. Gently ease the petals and stamens into an attractive shape.

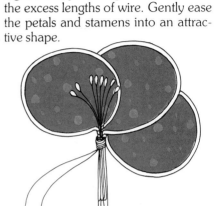

6 Bend and trim the stem wires to the required length, and bind them with green gutta tape. If any leaves are to be added, they can be bound in at this stage. Finally, arrange the flowers into the desired shape.

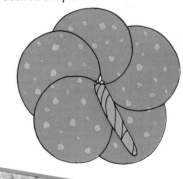

Flowered hat

Wired flowers are the perfect way to turn a plain straw hat into one which would be suitable for anything from a garden party to a formal wedding.

You will need: a straw hat; two tubes, one 3cm in diameter and one 2cm in diameter; small amounts of fabric, including white moiré, white broderie anglaise, yellow satin, white lace, black lace, blue felt, tartan cotton, red spot cotton, gold cotton, gold print cotton and natural hessian; artificial stamens in pearl, pink and yellow; cotton-covered flowermaking wire in white and green, and sewing thread.

Make wire forms from the white and green wire, enough for twenty flowers. Vary the shapes and sizes of these, and use the wire colour to contrast or blend with the chosen fabrics.

When the flowers are complete, trim the stem wires to 3cm. There is no need to cover these with tape, as the stems will not show. Bend the stems at right angles to each flower, and lay them round the brim of the hat, balancing out the shapes, colours and sizes in a pleasing way.

Use a long needle with a double length of fine sewing thread, or sewing silk, to make a couple of stitches round each flower stem and through the straw hat. Carry the thread through on the inside of the hat, making stitches not longer than 7cm, and secure each flower in this way. Finally, pull the individual flowers into attractive shapes.

Flower making accessories

Flower-making materials and accessories like leaves and stamens are now available in a range to suit most needs.

1 Stem wire This generally has a cotton covering in natural colours. The white can be coloured if necessary. Thicker, stronger wire is also available, usually in a metallic finish.

2 Binding wire This is like fine fuse wire, and is used to hold bunches of stems or petals together, or to hold leaves in place before the stems are covered with tape.

3 Floral tape This is a sticky-backed paper tape, available in natural colours, and is used to wrap round stems.

4 Leaves Choices include holly, ivy and beech leaves. These are usually paper-backed satin. Some are double sided, and two tone satin. Fancy leaves come in colours like red, pink and mauve, and silver foil.

5 Calyx flower backs Available in matt or shiny green, these have a central hole through which the flower stem is pushed.

6 Stamens and berries Choose from exotic and natural shapes, from tiny pearl and frosted stamens in bright colours, to realistic daisy centres and hammerseed stamens.

7 Small pliers These are necessary for bending, shaping and cutting wire.

Stencilled hat

Decorate a plain straw hat with a border of dragonflies stencilled on to the brim using brightly coloured permanent felt-tip pens.

You will need: a straw hat with a brim, permanent felt-tip pens in a range of different colours, 1.30m of 3cm-wide green satin ribbon, small green glass beads, matching thread, tracing paper, a small piece of thin card and a sharp craft knife.

Trace the dragonfly motif from the page and transfer it to thin card. Carefully cut out body, tail and wing sections using a sharp craft knife to make the stencil.

Using the stencil, mark the outlines of the dragonfly round the hat brim, using green for the body and tail sections and different colours for the wings. Turn the stencil round, use it in reverse and overlap one dragonfly sightly over another to achieve a variety of shapes.

Colour in the body, tail and wings in the same colours as the outlines. Sew two beads to each side of the front of the body on each dragonfly to make the eyes.

Tie the ribbon round the hat and knot it neatly at the back. Snip into the ends of the ribbon to make a V-shape and catchstitch the lower edge to the hat all round to secure.

Hat trims

There is an enormous range of hat trims to choose from, so when you buy a new outfit, look at your hats and decide whether they need re-trimming to match.

1 Ostrich pompon This pompon, made from the fronds of the ostrich feather, makes a beautiful trimming for a special hat.

2 Feather mounts Mounts are made by binding a variety of different feathers together to give a formal or sporty trimming ideal for winter hats in tweeds and velvets.

3 Single partridge feather This is a stylish and traditional trimming for a tweed hat.

4 Large single bloom This exquisite silk rose will put the finishing touch to a large summer beret made in organdie or silk.

5 Small single blooms These small polyester blooms can be used singly, or put together to form a cluster of different colours.

6 Clusters Small clusters of various flowers are available. Wild roses made in organdie and silk (below), and daisies and tiny flowers made in cotton (below and left) are ideal for summer hats and children's berets. Velvet clusters are more suitable for medium- to heavy-weight fabrics.

7 Velvet tubing This is ideal for soft bows and makes an effective trimming on velvet berets. Tubing can be bought in a limited colour range, or made in the hat fabric.

8 Satin ribbons These are ideal for flat bows. Choose a width to match the width of the headband and buy enough to go all the way round and tie at one side.

9 Velvet ribbon This is available in wide and narrow widths and makes a useful trimming for many heavier-weight fabrics.

10 Grosgrain ribbon This is a stiff ribbon which usually has a matt finish. Metallic grosgrain is also available for a fancy finish.

Chapter 5

F·O·O·T·W·E·A·R

If you have always looked at shoes and socks from a conventional angle, now is the time to revolutionize your thinking. It is just as easy to dress up plain shoes or add a personal touch to purchased socks as it is to accessorize a simple dress; so instead of buying footwear to match your outfits, experiment with some of the ideas here. Paint shoes and socks to add zest to your sportswear; splash them with gold, glitter and sequins for party wear, or use your embroidery skills to decorate them in colours which echo your clothes, and if you have time to spare, treat yourself to the luxury of handknitted socks or sandals made from crocheted ribbon.

Shoe trims

With a little imagination – and very little effort – you can revolutionize your shoe rack, turning simple pumps into party shoes and lace-ups into works of art; even boots and wellies get a new, exciting look.

1 Stick motifs cut from braid to black pumps and echo the shapes with gold paint, or simply use the paint to make random marks.

2 Bind a pipecleaner with glitter thread and wind it around a hairpin. Bend the pipecleaner in half and trim each end with a bead. Slipstitch it in place, adding curls of coloured gift ribbon.

3 Make a collection of beads in different shapes and colours and stitch them to fabric shoes.

1

4 Stuff fabric pumps with tissue paper, lightly mark your design in pencil, then fill it in with fabric paint or shoe dye.

4

5

5 Develop an eye for possible clip-on motifs and keep a collection made from fabric, ribbon, paper, sequin-waste or whatever takes your fancy.

6 Paint heels and toes with glue then sprinkle on glitter to match your party dress, or thread running stitches through fabric holes.

6

7 Transform cheap pumps with sequins and couch-stitched rays, or
punch giant eyelet holes and thread
them with a ribbon to suit your mood
and your clothes.

8 Cut the fabric uppers from mules
and, leaving 1cm turnings all round,
cut new uppers from canvas (12 holes
to 2.5cm). Embroider the canvas
pieces with assorted wools and stitches. Glue the turnings to the wrong side
and back each piece with felt. Slide the
edges of the canvaswork between the
upper and lower soles of the slippers
and glue them securely in place.

9 Splash lace-ups with random flower motifs or geometric designs.

10 Wrap braid around plain boots and glue or catch-stitch it in place, adding other trims if desired. Punch holes around the tops and thread them with glitter yarn.

11 Stick paper shapes to a child's wellies and make them more rainproof by covering them with small pieces of sticky-backed plastic.

Ribbon sandals

These pretty sandals are made from fine ribbon, with raffia for the inner sole and garden string for the outer sole, but they could also be crocheted in leather or suede thonging, raffia, or rag strips, or other fancy yarns.

You will need: two spools of 1.5m polyester ribbon (A); two skeins of rayon raffia (B); one ball of coarse brown garden string (C); 2m of narrow corded gold ribbon; 3mm, 4mm and 6mm crochet hooks, and two rubber soles (if these are difficult to obtain, cover the rope sole of the sandal with a thick layer of rubber glue to form a firm, water-tight base).

Tension
20½ sts and 21 rows to 10cm over double crochet using the ribbon and 3mm hook

Note: Wherever possible, work over the loose ends to save darning in spare yarn once the pieces are completed.

For the toe section (make two): using 3mm hook and A, make 35ch.
1st row: 1dc into 2nd ch from hook, 1dc into each ch to end, turn. 34dc.
Work 5 more rows dc.
Next row: 1ss into each dc to end. Fasten off.

For the heels (make two): using 3mm hook and A, make 27ch.
1st row: 1dc into 2nd ch from hook, 1dc into each ch to end, turn. 26 sts.

Work 7 more rows dc. Fasten off. With RS of work facing, rejoin A to lower corner at side edge.
Next row: 1ch, 6dc up side edge, 3dc into corner, 1dc into each st across top, 3dc into corner, 7dc down side edge and into final corner, turn.
Work one more row dc all round, working 1dc into each st and 3dc into each corner, turn.
Next row: 1ss into each dc all round. Fasten off.

For the inner sole (make two): using 4mm hook and B, make 6ch.
1st row: 1dc into 2nd ch from hook, 1dc into each ch to end, turn. 5dc.
2nd row: 1ch, 1dc into first st, 1dc into each dc to end, 2dc into turning chain, turn. 7dc.
3rd row: As 2nd. 9dc.
Work 7 more rows dc without shaping, adjusting length between heel and instep at this point if required.

Shape instep
Next row: 1ch, 2dc tog, dc to last 3 sts, 2dc tog, 1dc into turning chain, turn. Work 5 rows dc without shaping.

Shape foot
1st row: 1ch, 1dc into each st to end, 2dc into turning chain, turn.
2nd row: 1ch, 1dc into first st, 1dc into each st to end, 2dc into turning chain, turn.
Work 3 rows dc without shaping, adjusting length as before if required.

Shape toe
1st row: As 2nd row of foot shaping. Work 3 rows dc without shaping.
Next row: 1ch, dc to last 3 sts, 2dc tog, 1dc into turning chain, turn.
Next row: 1ch, 2dc tog, dc to last 3 sts, 2dc tog, 1dc into turning chain, turn.
Work 6 rows dc without shaping, adjusting length if required as before. Dec one st at each end of next and foll row in same way as before. 4sts.
Next row: 1ch, (2dc tog) twice. Fasten off.

Edging
With RS of work facing, rejoin A at corner of heel using 4mm hook.
Next round: 1ch, 1dc into same place as ch, cont working dc all round sole, working 1dc into each st or row end

and 2dc into corners each time to keep sole flat. Join with a ss to first ch.
Work 1 more round dc in same way. Fasten off.

For the rope sole (make two): using 6mm hook and C, make 19ch.
1st round: 1dc into 2nd ch from hook and each ch to end, 3dc into last ch, turn and work 1dc into other side of each st a long base ch to end. Join with a ss to first ch.
2nd round: 1ch, 1dc into st at base of ch, 2dc into next st, 1dc into each st along side, 2dc into each st at end to turn, 1dc into each st down 2nd side. Join with a ss to first ch.
3rd round: 1ch, 1dc into st at base of ch, 2dc into each of next 2 sts, 1dc into each of next 8dc, ss across 5 sts at instep, 1dc into each of next 5sts, 2dc into each of next 4 sts round heel, 1dc into each of next 5 sts, ss across 5 sts at instep, 1dc into each st at end. Join with a ss to first ch.
Fasten off.
With RS of work facing, rejoin C to first dc after instep slip stitches.
Next round: 1ss into next st then each st all round toe to last dc before slip stitches at other side. Fasten off.

Pull rope sole firmly into shape so that it lies flat, darning in loose ends securely on wrong side. Pin raffia sole to right side of rope sole, pinning ribbon toe piece in place at same time. Pin toe piece at slight angle to follow shape of foot, and try on. Using A, oversew inner sole neatly to rope sole, taking A through outer loop only of each border stitch on raffia sole, and working through both thicknesses when toe piece is reached. Using B, sew 2 or 3 rows of running stitches down length of foot as neatly as possible to hold inner sole flat against rope sole, making sure the stitches do not show on under side of rope sole, to prevent them from wearing.

Oversew heel section in place, making sure centre of ribbon heel is lined up with centre of sole. Thread narrow gold ribbon through top of heel section taking ribbon in and out of each stitch. Knot ribbon firmly at each end and cut close to knot. Glue rubber sole cut to shape to base of rope sole.

Winter warmers

Forget chilly feet this winter — just snuggle your toes in these cosy foot-warmers with their pretty crochet trim.

For shoes size 37-38 you will need: 20cm of 140cm-wide acrylic jersey fleece or a blanket remnant, 25cm of 90cm-wide cotton lining fabric, one 25g ball of double knitting yarn, scraps of contrasting yarn, squared paper, and a crochet hook.

To make the pattern, scale up diagram to full size, using squared graph paper. With fabric in single thickness, cut two soles and two uppers from both fleecy and lining fabric. (To alter the size, draw round foot and scale the pattern up or down accordingly.)

To work crochet edgings, with right sides facing, pierce crochet hook through fabric 1cm from outside edge. Draw yarn through and make a slip loop on crochet hook, securing with a knot on the wrong side. Work 2ch. Insert hook through fabric 1cm along from starting point, draw through loop, yrh, draw through both loops on hook, work 1 ch. Continue crochet edging in this way all round outside edges. Fasten ends of yarn neatly.

To embroider flowers, mark the centre positions with a single cross stitch in contrast yarn. With main shade, work four petals in detached chain stitches Fasten neatly on the wrong side.

Alternatively, you may prefer to attach tiny bows made from contrast yarn.

For the linings, turn 1cm to the wrong side on all raw edges and press. With wrong sides facing, slipstitch lining pieces to soles and uppers at base of crochet.

With right sides facing, join centre back seam of upper by oversewing crochet edgings together, using main shade of yarn. On the right side, pin upper to sole, easing in gradually and oversew edgings together.

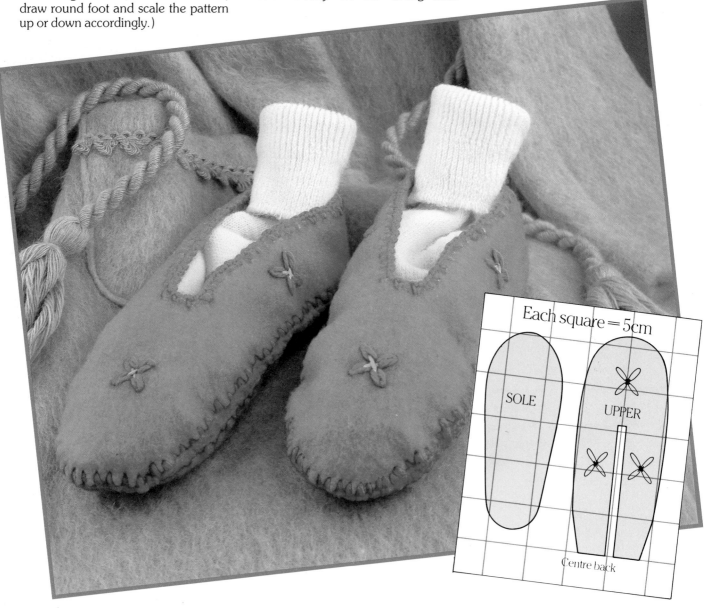

Each square = 5cm

SOLE

UPPER

Centre back

Slipper socks

Comfortable slipper socks in strong, bold colours keep legs and feet warm in style.

For socks to fit 30cm to 35cm calves you will need: two balls of chunky in main colour (A); two balls in each of two contrast colours (B) and (C), one pair each of 4½mm and 5½mm needles, and approximately 30cm x 30cm of leather for the sole.

Tension
14 sts and 17 rows to 10cm over st st on 5½mm needles.

Using 4½mm needles and B, cast on 40 sts and work 10 rows in K2, P2 rib. Change to 5½mm needles and patt.
1st row K3A, *1C, 1B, 2A, 1B, 2A, 1C, 1B*, 16A, rep from * to * once more, 3A.
2nd row P3A, *1C, 1B, 2A, 1C, 2A, 1C, 1B*, 16A, rep from * to * once more, 3A.
Rep 1st and 2nd rows once more.
5th row K1C, 1B, *1C, 3B, 1C, 1B, 1C, 4B,* (1C, 1B) 7 times, rep from * to * once more, 1C, 1B.
6th row P1C, 1B, *1C, 2B, (1C, 1B) twice, 1C, 3B,* (1C, 1B) 7 times, rep from * to * once more, 1C, 1B.
Rep 5th and 6th rows once more.
9th-16th rows Rep 1st-2nd rows 4 times more.

These 16 rows form the patt. Cont in patt until work measures 50cm from beg, ending with wrong side row. (Length may be adjusted here.)

Shape toe Keeping patt correct:
Next row (K1, K2 tog, K14, sl 1, K1, psso, K1) twice. 36 sts.
Next row P.
Next row (K1, K2 tog, K12, sl 1, K1, psso, K1) twice. 32 sts.
Next row P.
Next row (K1, K2 tog, K10, sl 1, K1, psso, K1) twice. 28 sts.
Next row (P1, P2 tog tbl, P8, P2 tog, P1) twice. 24 sts.
Next row (K1, K2 tog, K6, sl 1, K1, psso, K1) twice. 20 sts.
Next row (P1, P2 tog tbl, P4, P2 tog, P1) twice. 16 sts.
Next row (K1, K2 tog, K2, sl 1, K1, psso, K1) twice. 12 sts.
Cast off.

Pin out and press according to instructions on ball band. Fold rib in half on to wrong side and slipstitch down.
Fold socks lengthways and work an invisible seam down the front of the leg and toe section, leaving the ribbed channel at top of leg open.

Make four pompons (see page 80)

using oddments of yarn. Cut 2 x 60cm lengths of each colour and thread three strands through the ribbed channel of each sock top. Sew a pompon to each end of cord.

Trace around each foot on to the leather. Cut out each sole and stitch on to underside of sock, beginning at the toe end. Soft leather may be cut wider and brought up sides of foot.

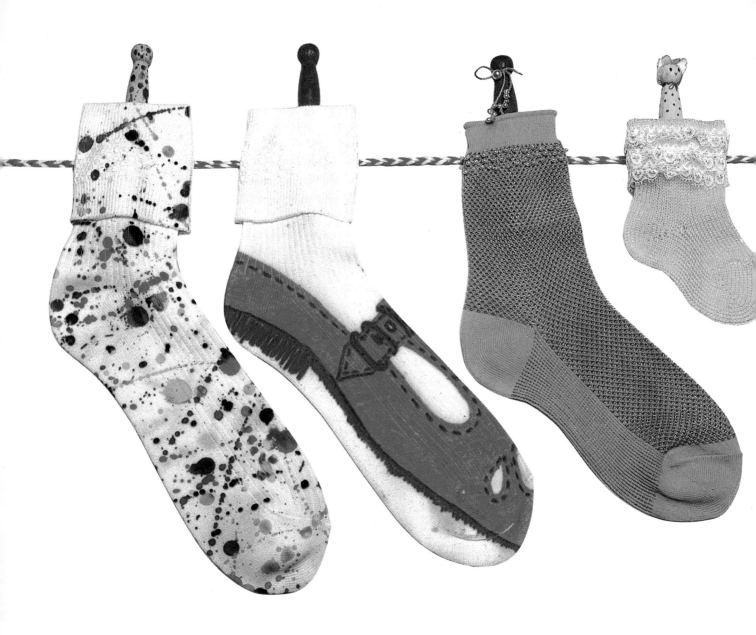

Socks for fun

Socks are very much back in fashion as an accessory, so try out different ways of giving them an individual touch.

For the splash happy and sandal socks you will need: purchased socks in synthetic fibres such as nylon or acrylic (transfer printing only works on synthetic fibres), transfer paints and brush (splash happy socks) or transfer crayons (sandal socks), paper, an iron and ironing board.

Splash happy socks
Spread newspaper over the working area then, using a paint brush, splash transfer paints over a large sheet of white paper. Leave the paper to dry thoroughly then cut it into four.

Sandwich each sock between two pieces of paper and press well on both sides with a warm iron. Check that the dye has transferred sufficiently and remove the paper.

Sandal socks
Place one sock on a sheet of paper and draw round the outline. Sketch half a sandal on this paper pattern and colour it in with transfer crayons. Sketch the second half of the sandal for the other side of this sock and make a matching pair of patterns for the second sock of your pair so that they will fit left and right feet.

Paint and fix, following the instructions given for the Splash happy socks.

Beaded socks
Decorate a purchased sock with pearly beads. You could even use them to pick out the design of a patterned or knitted sock.

Baby socks
Trim purchased baby socks with 50cm of gathered baby lace to make a lovely little present for a newborn infant.

Handknitted Fair Isle socks

These socks will really stand out from the mass-produced crowd, making the perfect complement to stylish country clothes.

You will need: three 50g balls of 4 ply superwash in main colour (A); oddments in contrast colours (B), (C), (D) and (E), and a set of four 2¾ knitting needles pointed at both ends.

Tension

36 sts and 42 rows to 10cm over st st

Using 3 of the set of four 2¾mm needles and A, cast on 28 sts on to each needle. 84·sts. Using the 4th needle work 6 rounds in K2, P2 rib. Commence patt.

1st round K and A.
2nd round *K5A, 1B, rep from * to end.
3rd round *K1C, 3A, 3C, 3A, 2C, rep from * to end.
4th round *K2C, 1D, rep from * to end.
5th round K in D.
6th round K in B.
7th round K in D.
8th round *K1E, 1D, rep from * to end.
9th round *K2E, (1A, 1E) 3 times, 1A, 2E, 1A, rep from * to end.
10th round *K3B, (1A, 1B) twice, 1A, 3B, 1A, rep from * to end.
11th round *K5D, 1C, rep from * to end.
12th round As 10th round.
13th round As 9th round.
14th round As 8th round.
15th round As 7th round.
16th round As 6th round.
17th round As 5th round.
18th round As 4th round.
19th round As 3rd round.
20th round As 2nd round.
Cont in A only. K in rounds until work measures 15cm from the beg.

Shape leg

Next round K1, K2 tog, K to last 3 sts, sl 1, K1, psso, K1, K4 rounds.
Rep last 5 rounds 3 times more. 76 sts. Cont without shaping until work measures 40cm from beg. Cut yarn.

Divide for heel

Sl first 18 sts and last 20 sts of round on to one needle for heel. Divide rem 38 sts on to 2 needles and leave for instep.

Shape heel

With RS of work facing, rejoiñ yarn to sts for heel.
1st row Sl 1, K to end.
2nd row *Sl 1, P1, rep from * to end.
Rep the last 2 rows 14 times more, then the 1st row again.

Turn heel

Next row P21, P2 tog, P1, turn.
Next row K6, K2 tog, K1, turn.
Next row P7, P2 tog, P1, turn.
Next row K8, K2 tog, K1, turn.
Cont in this way until 22 sts rem, ending with a K row.

Working on to same needle; K up 16 sts along side of heel, (Mark the end st), on to a free needle, K the 38 sts of instep, then on to another needle K up 16 sts along other side of heel and K to marker at end of round. Now, there should be a total of 38 sts on 1st needle, and 27 sts on each of the 2nd and 3rd needles.

Shape instep

1st round K.
2nd round K38, K1, sl 1, K1, psso, K to last 3 sts, K2 tog, K1.
Rep the last 2 rounds until 72 sts rem. Cont without shaping until foot measures 20cm from back of heel.

Shape toe

K next st of round, then sl last st on first needle on to 3rd needle, so arranging sts with 36 sts on 1st needle and 18 sts on 2nd and 3rd needles.
1st round K1, K2 tog, K to last 3 sts on 1st needle, sl 1, K1, psso, K1, from 2nd needle, K1, K2 tog, K to end, from 3rd needle, K to last 3 sts, sl 1, K1, psso, K1.
Next round K.
Rep last 2 rounds until 24 sts rem. Sl sts from 2nd needle on to 3rd needle. Graft or cast off sts from 2 needles together. Press lightly.

Chapter 6

J·E·W·E·L·L·E·R·Y

Jewellery does not have to be expensive to add style and sparkle to your clothes, and if you make your own then you can afford to ring the changes more often, choosing a necklace, brooch, earrings or hair ornament to put the finishing touch to an outfit.

A small beaded brooch makes a colourful accent on a plain dress, a plaited or twisted necklace can add interest to a simple neckline or accentuate a sun tun; earrings can quickly be made from sequins or scraps of fabric to echo the colours or motifs of a summery dress or skirt, and a pretty ornament draws attention to your hair and eyes.

Fabric jewellery

Mock jewellery is fun to make – it can be shaped from an endless variety of materials like soft leather, plastic, sparkling metallic threads, beads and other exotic fabrics, to suit every possible occasion.

Leather necklace

You will need: a 65cm x 5cm strip of leather each in red, blue and green; a 65cm x 5mm strip of yellow leather, cut with pinking shears; two tulip-shaped cup holders; a small chain with clasp, buttons or beads to decorate, strong thread, and a spearpoint machine needle.

Adjust the machine to a medium-long stitch with right sides facing, stitch the long seam of each 65cm x 5cm leather strip and turn them right side out.

Using strong thread bind the four strips together at one end. Plait the three wide strips and wind the zigzag one loosely around them. Bind the second end. Loosely knot centre of plait and stitch on buttons or beads for decoration.

Fit a tulip-shaped cup holder and a short length of chain with clasp to either end of the leather necklace.

Glitter and gold

You will need: 30cm strands of fine metallic knitting or embroidery threads in assorted colours; two tulip-shaped cup holders for covering ends of threads; forty 3mm gold beads; ten 1cm gold beads (with large holes in the centres for threading with metallic yarns); five 12mm white beads; a beading needle; strong thread; adhesive, and a suitable clasp.

Knot the strands of metallic yarns and thread at either end. Using a beading needle and strong thread, stitch through the knot at one end of the metallic strands. Thread a tulip cup over knot and follow with twenty 3mm gold beads. Knot thread to one end of the clasp and secure it with a spot of clear adhesive.

Stitch through the knot at the other end of the metallic strands and thread with ten 1cm gold beads. Pull the beads into place over the metallic strands and position them neatly as shown.

Part the metallic strands slightly and insert a white bead into every alternate section. Rearrange the metallic strands and gold beads as shown above. Secure the position of the white beads with a few spots of glue.

Stitch through the knot at the second end of the metallic strands and finish the same as before.

Bag of sweets brooch

Make a small bag from clear PVC and adhesive tape. Fill with sweets made from felt wrapped in PVC and bound at either end with brightly coloured sewing thread. Cut the top edge of the bag with pinking shears, gather and tie as shown. Attach a safety pin to centre back of brooch as a fastening.

Flower necklace

You will need: 50cm each of black and purple satin bias binding; 20cm of 90cm-wide cream silk or polyester satin fabric and 20cm of 90cm-wide of wadding; 12cm x 4cm of black felt; 50cm of gold knitting yarn; 24cm of string; black wool and sewing threads in red, black and purple; fabric paints in red, white, black and purple; two tulip-shaped metallic cup holders and a necklace clasp; tracing paper, and loose cotton wool.

Cut six 10cm x 12cm pieces, eight 4cm squares and three 5cm squares from satin fabric. Cut three 3cm x 4cm pieces of black felt and cut a 1cm deep fringe along one 4cm edge of each of the pieces.

Following manufacturer's instructions, colour four of the 10cm x 12cm pieces and four 4cm squares with red fabric paint. Dilute the paint slightly for a shaded effect. Paint two 10cm x 12cm and four 4cm squares purple and three 5cm squares black. Allow the painted areas to dry thoroughly and fix with a hot iron.

Trace off and transfer 36 flower petal shapes to the large pieces of fabric and eight small flowers to the 4cm squares. Sandwich wadding between two layers of each coloured fabric and straight stitch around the outlined shapes. Using a small closely-spaced zigzag stitch and matching threads, work around each stitched outline. Cut out the individual flower petals and decorate the inside of each one

with a few light strokes of white fabric paint. Cut out the small flowers and paint the centres black.

Place a small ball of cotton wool in the centre of each black satin square. Tie tightly with thread and tie an 8cm length of string to each one.

Wrap felt fringes around flower centres and tie tightly with thread. Handsew petals around each flower centre. Bind strings tightly with black wool.

Plait the satin bindings and the gold thread and tie tightly at each end. Stitch a tulip-shaped cup holder over each end of the plait. Sew the necklace clasp in place. Push the bound ends of string through the plait, positioning flowers as shown. Bend the stems back on themselves, stitch with cotton thread and bind in place with black wool.

Using black thread stitch one small red and purple flower to each side of the three main flowers.

Knitted chain necklace

Link up strands of knitted colour for this crazy necklace.

You will need: one 50g ball of DK in each of five contrasting colours; a pair of 4mm knitting needles, and one press stud.

Tension
12 sts and 15 rows to 5cm over st st on 4mm needles.

Using 4mm needles and colour A, cast on 10 sts.
Work in st st for 17cm.
Cast off.
Work two strips of each colour in the same way.

Do not press. Allow the edges of each strip to curl in towards the centre. Using oddments of matching yarn, stitch together the short ends of one strip. Slip the second strip through the first loop to form a chain link and stitch the ends as before. Continue working in this way to the last link, which should be joined with a press stud. You could ring the changes by using knitting yarns in variegated colours.

114

Knitted & crocheted jewellery

Knitted and crocheted jewellery is quick to make and fun to wear, so liven up casual clothes with jewellery made from colourful plastic tubing and beads, or knit in black and gold to team up with evening wear.

For the crocheted jewellery you will need: five 56cm strands of 2mm-diameter plastic tubing, six leaf beads in colours (A) and (B), 13 gold ring beads, one screw clasp, a pair of earrings, one hair slide, and a 3.50mm crochet hook.

For the knitted jewellery you will need: one ball of fine gold crochet cotton, one ball of fine black crochet cotton, one pair of gold earrings, two gold screw clasps, and one pair of 2¼mm knitting needles.

Crocheted jewellery

Necklace Leaving 14cm, make 3ch, thread gold bead (tgb), 10ch, tgb, *3ch, thread leaf bead (tbl), 3ch, tgb, * join next length, rep from * to * twice, 10ch, tgb, 3ch.
Leaving 14cm end, cast off.
Tgb, tie on clasp, leaving 10cm single strand. Rep for other end of necklace.

Earrings ** Leaving 7cm, make 8ch. Ss into first ch. Leave 7cm end, cast off. Pass both ends through centre ch. Tgb up both ends, thread one leaf bead up one strand and another up the second strand. Pass both strands back through centre ch, leaving leaf beads at front. Tie in ends. ** Thread earring. Rep for second earring.

Hair slide Rep from ** to ** as for earrings. Attach to both ends of slide.

Knitted jewellery

Necklace Using A, cast on 25 sts. *Work 8 rows in st st. Change to B. Work 6 rows in st st.* Rep from * to * 12 times more. Using A, work 8 rows in st st. Cast off.
With A, gather each end and sew screw clasp on to both ends.

Bracelet Rep from * to * as for necklace, 4 times. Change to A and work 8 rows st st. Cast off. Finish as for necklace.

Earrings Using A, cast on 10 sts. Work 8 rows in st st. Change to B. Work 6 rows in st st. Change to A. Work 8 rows in st st. Cast off. Sew ends together and thread earring.

Ring Using A, cast on 10 sts. Work 2 rows in st st. Change to B. Work 2 rows in st st. Rep last 4 rows, 4 times. Using A, work 2 rows st st. Cast off. Sew ends together.

Shell necklace

Make this lovely exotic necklace from plaited cords with shells, coins and hanging beads clustered along the centre.

You will need: 1m each of narrow cord in purple, silver, lilac and white; 2m of narrow cord in pink; 1m of Russia braid in white/silver; a selection of shells, coins and beads with ready drilled holes; small round open-ended links; sewing thread, and small pliers and tweezers.

Make a plait using two of the 1m lengths of narrow cord (purple and silver), and half the 2m length of narrow cord (pink). Knot ends together and trim neatly.

Sew one end of all the remaining cords and braid to this plait 12cm from one end, bind thread round and round to cover ends and fasten securely.

Plait together, using Russia braid as one string, the first plait as the second string and the three remaining narrow cords (lilac, white and pink) together as the third. When this new plait measures 45cm, sew all cords and braid together firmly. Trim off excess

length of all cords except the remaining 12cm of first plait, and bind thread round to cover ends as before.

Along one edge of the middle 20cm of the large plait, fasten the shells, coins and beads: using small pliers and tweezers, open the round links, thread on a bead and close over a single braid. In order to balance your design, it is best to position the larger ornaments along the plait first and then fill in with the smaller ones, arranging the shapes in a pleasing way. To wear, tie the ends of the small plait together in a simple knot.

Paper beads

These pretty paper beads are fun to make and can be painted in any colour combinations to accessorize your clothes perfectly.

You will need: one large sheet cartridge paper; PVA glue; acrylic paints in red, yellow and blue; watercolour brushes; 2m narrow braid or Paris binding; a craft knife; a metal ruler; and a 4.50mm or 5.00mm crochet hook.

Mark out strips on cartridge paper to the size shown and then cut out using a sharp craft knife and a metal ruler. Cut about 40 strips for both the necklace and bracelet.

Lay one strip of paper on a pad of newspaper and spread one side even-ly with glue. Starting with the wider end, roll the strip round the crochet hook, close to the end. Keep rolling firmly and evenly until you reach the end of the paper and then carefully slide the bead off the hook. Repeat with remaining strips and leave the beads to dry hard.

Once dry, paint each bead with a base coat of red, blue or yellow (or other colours, as desired). Hold each bead on the end of a pencil or brush as you paint it, stand on its end on newspaper and then leave to dry for several hours.

Next paint random flecks of colour on to the beads in the two contrasting colours. Paint with one colour at a time and leave to dry between colours.

When all the beads are dry, thread them on to the braid; alternating the colours. (To make threading easier, dip one end of the braid into glue and leave it to dry.) Make a single or double knot between each bead to keep in place. When you reach the required length, cut the braid, leaving enough to tie the ends together.

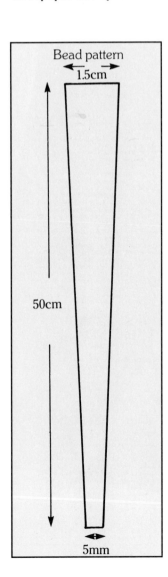

Bead pattern

1.5cm

50cm

5mm

Earrings for fun

These stunning earrings are simple to make and fun to wear. Mix beads, sequins and sumptuous fabrics for an original result.

For the leaf earrings you will need: two silver hooks; two red, pink and green leaf sequins; small silver beads; silver or light grey thread, and clear adhesive.

For the bow earrings you will need: two gold hooks; 10cm of pink silk; gold lamé and paper-backed bonding; gold thread and clear adhesive.

Leaf earrings

Thread both ends of a length of thread through the eye of a beading needle. Thread one bead and pass the needle through the end loop to secure.

Thread seven more beads and then thread a red, pink and green leaf sequin with a silver bead between each one. Thread seven beads once more and pass the needle through the very first bead to make a loop.

Thread two more beads and then pass the needle through the earring hook. Make several buttonhole stitches around the hook, cut the thread close to last stitch and secure stitches with a spot of clear adhesive. Repeat for second earring.

Bow earrings

Bond the pink silk to the gold lamé with double-sided paper-backed bonding, and cut out two pieces measuring 6cm x 4cm. Fold both pieces into a concertina, pressing at each fold with a very hot iron.

Using matching coloured sewing thread, catch the centre with a few stitches, wind the thread round the outside and bring the needle out on the pink side. Thread four gold beads, take the needle back through first three and bring out on the gold side. Thread six more beads and then attach to earring hook as before.

Embroidered earrings

Fan yourself without raising a finger - a pair of delicate, pretty fan-shaped earrings, that are both quick to embroider and fun to wear.

To make a pair of earrings 7cm x 4.5cm, you will need: 10cm x 22cm of single canvas, 22 holes to 2.5cm; 10cm x 15cm piece of deep pink satin lining fabric; 30cm of iron-on bonding; Anchor stranded embroidery cotton in orange (0324), pale green (0240), dull yellow (0311), flesh pink (06), pale turquoise blue (0167), deep pink (078) and rust brown (0352); deep pink sewing thread; small glass beads, in pink and blue, and two earring wires.

Using three strands of embroidery cotton, work the fan design in tent stitch, following the chart. Take care to keep an even tension; if necessary, place the canvas in a small frame.

Stitch the beads on top of the embroidery, scattering them over the right-hand side of each earring.

Using iron-on bonding, bond the satin lining to the back of each earring, wrong sides together. Using deep pink sewing thread, machine zigzag stitch round the outline of each fan shape, stitching through all three layers.

Attach earring wires to the top of each earring.

1sq = 1 stitch

Tent stitch

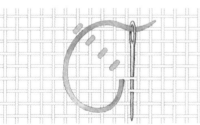

1 Bring the needle through to the front of the canvas and insert it to the right of the intersection of threads above. Take the needle behind two horizontal threads of canvas so that it emerges at the bottom of the next stitch.

2 Work the first row from top left to bottom right and the second from bottom right to top left. Bring out the needle and insert it to the right of the intersection of threads above. Take it horizontally behind two vertical threads, ready for the next switch.

Strawberry brooch

Add a sparkle to your wardrobe with this colourful strawberry brooch worked in rows of glass beads to catch the limelight.

You will need: one box each of bright red, dark red and green beads; 26 gold beads; small square of red felt; red and green thread; brooch back; clear adhesive, and paper for the template.

Trace the motif on to paper and cut it out. Lay the template on the felt and draw round the outline. Fill in leaf outlines by hand and mark dots for the positions of gold beads.

Starting at the bottom of each strawberry, sew beads in rows from left to right and right to left, by threading a bead, taking a small stitch into the felt and threading the next bead. Thread gold beads at positions marked and use dark red beads to give a shadow beside the main strawberry, where the two strawberries meet. Finish with green beads at tops. Fasten threads securely on wrong side of felt.

When all the beading is complete, apply a thin layer of clear adhesive to the back of the felt, taking it right up to the outer edges of the motif. Allow to dry. Cut round the edge of the motif.

Stick the beaded motif on to a second layer of felt to neaten the back and allow it to dry. Trim the felt to shape and sew the brooch back in position towards the centre top of the brooch, using tiny overcasting stitches.

Scarf brooch

Brighten up a plain sweater with this original brooch with miniature needles and scarf, or use it as an unusual gift for a keen knitter.

You will need: one ball of blue pearl cotton No. 5, 2mm needles, two cocktail sticks and wooden beads to fit, clear adhesive and a brooch pin or small gold safety pin.

Using 2mm needles, cast on 8 sts. K20 rows in g st.

To make the needles, clip the point from one end of each of the cocktail sticks and apply a drop of clear adhesive. Thread a wooden bead on each stick and allow it to dry for about a minute.

Transfer the stitches to one wooden needle and secure the second needle in place by winding the thread around the two needles to make a little ball of yarn.

Take the thread to the back of the scarf and use it to attach a brooch pin or small gold safety pin by stitching invisibly into the back of the knitting.

Cut the thread. Darn in the end on cast-on edge.

Cut 8cm lengths of pearl cotton for the fringe. Fold each length in half and in half again and thread the centre fold through a darning needle. Take needle through one stitch on the cast-on edge and thread the four loose ends through the resulting loop to secure. Pull the thread tight. Repeat along bottom of scarf and trim the fringe to 1.5cm.

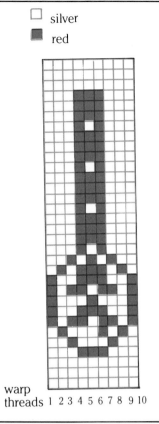

silver
red

warp threads 1 2 3 4 5 6 7 8 9 10

Beadwork hair slide

This pretty beadwork hair slide is made on a bead loom. Choose two contrasting colours to bring out the geometric pattern.

You will need: a bead loom pack containing a loom, beading needles, beeswax, thread and instructions; 1oz red beads; 1oz silver beads; 1 hair grip, and embroidery scissors.

Cut ten warp threads 36cm long, knot one end and pull it through the beeswax. Divide the threads in two and place five threads on each side of the metal screw on the top wooden roller. Wind the threads on by turning the wooden roller away from you until the other end can be knotted and placed on the other roller in the same way. Keep the threads smooth and even.

Place each thread between the spiral separators and make sure that 8cm of

the thread is wound round the bottom roller. Then tighten both rollers with the screw on the side of the loom.

Thread the beading needle to 70cm when doubled and knot it to the fourth warp thread from the left, close to the bottom roller.

Place beads in a small tin and pick up the first three red beads. Take the needle under the warp threads, place each bead beween two threads and bring the needle up straight after the seventh thread. Put it back through the beads again so they are secured from above.

Add beads according to the chart, placing them as before, and weave in the ends as you work. Repeat the middle section until it measures 15cm, ending on a row with a silver bead, and repeat the medallion pattern in reverse. Simply turn the chart upside

down and continue weaving. Turn the rollers gently as you work so that the finished piece winds underneath.

To join in new threads, weave the old thread back through a couple of rows and cut off in the middle of a row close to a bead. Weave in the new thread through a few rows until you reach the starting point. Wax each new thread before you begin.

To finish off, loosen the rollers and remove the work from the loom. Untie or cut the knots at each end and cut the warp threads at each side of the middle section at the centre of their length. Weave all the loose thread ends into the work and trim close to a bead to neaten.

Place the finished beadwork at the end of the hair grip; adjust length so that both ends can be seen, and fix it in your hair to make a pretty decoration.

Hair comb

Bring fashion and fantasy to your hair with this pretty comb and its colourful silk flowers.

You will need: scraps of red, blue and green fabric; lightweight wadding; two diamanté studs and claws; a clamp; a tortoise-shell hair comb, and thin card for templates.

Transfer the outline of the flower and leaf motifs on to thin card and cut out templates.

Cut two 5cm squares of fabric for each flower and leaf, sandwich small pieces of wadding in between and tack the layers together.

Position the templates on the padded fabric pieces and draw round the edge of each motif.

Machine stitch along the outline of each motif, using a close zigzag stitch and matching sewing thread. Cut out the shapes close to the stitching using sharp embroidery scissors. Machine stitch edges again with a slightly larger zigzag stitch. Clamp one diamanté stud to the centre of each flower.

Attach a length of matching sewing thread to each flower and leaf. Wind each one round the bar on the comb several times and apply a drop of clear adhesive to secure it in place, first arranging the flowers and leaves in a pleasing way. Use the photograph as a guide. Join the edges of different motifs with a few tiny stitches to complete the hair comb.

123

I·N·D·E·X